THE END OF LIFE AS WE KNOW IT

OUT OF GAS
USING UP FOSSIL FUELS

SHERRI MABRY GORDON

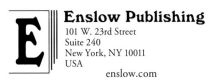

Enslow Publishing
101 W. 23rd Street
Suite 240
New York, NY 10011
USA
enslow.com

Published in 2016 by Enslow Publishing, LLC
101 W. 23rd Street, Suite 240, New York, NY 10011

Library of Congress Cataloging-in-Publication Data

Names: Gordon, Sherri Mabry.
Title: Out of gas: using up fossil fuels / Sherri Mabry Gordon.
Description: New York : Enslow Publishing, 2016. | Series: The end of life as we know it | Includes index.
Identifiers: ISBN 9780766073067 (library bound)
Subjects: LCSH: Fossil fuels--Juvenile literature. | Energy conservation--Juvenile literature. | Pollution--Juvenile literature.
Classification: LCC TP318.3 G67 2016 | DDC 333.8'2--dc23

Printed in the United States of America

To Our Readers: We have done our best to make sure all website addresses in this book were active and appropriate when we went to press. However, the author and the publisher have no control over and assume no liability for the material available on those websites or on any websites they may link to. Any comments or suggestions can be sent by e-mail to customerservice@enslow.com.

Portions of this book originally appeared in the book *Green and Clean Energy: What You Can Do.*

CONTENTS

"Don't stand there with the door open!" Most kids are used to hearing their parents tell them to shut the fridge and turn off the lights.

CHAPTER 1

WASTING AWAY

EVERYWHERE WE TURN WE ARE LOSING ENERGY.
Whether it is going up in a puff of smoke or leaking someplace, Americans waste energy every day. And the problem is, we don't have an endless supply. Eventually it will be gone for good if we don't do something about it today.

There are several problems with wasting energy, says Christy Radanof, a mother of two who owns a company that sells environmentally friendly cleaning products in Pickerington, Ohio. Aside from the fact that it costs money that could be spent on other things, energy waste causes us to use up our energy supply faster than we should and it pollutes our environment, she says.[1]

Radanof, who who is also a substitute teacher, says she wants young people to understand that changing simple things can have a big impact. For this reason, Radanof has not only developed a green program at the elementary school where she works, but she also has been teaching her own children how to conserve energy.

"They're kind of like my green police now, blowing the whistle on me every time I forget something," she says. "So, for example, they will walk by us and remind us if we leave the water on for any length of time.

Whether we are rinsing dishes or brushing our teeth, the water is off until we need it—not running the whole time."

But conserving water is not the family's only focus. The Radanofs are always looking for opportunities to conserve energy. For example, they bring their own bags to the grocery, combine their errands to save gasoline, and replace their lightbulbs with LCD bulbs.

They also recycle as much as they can. In fact, recycling has become a family activity. Radanof says they have even made it into a game to see if they really need to put the garbage can at the curb each week. Sometimes they are able to go more than two weeks without putting the garbage can out because they reuse or recycle the majority of their waste.

"The little choice of 'Do I throw it in the trash can or do I just take it to the recycle bin,' is training your brain," Radanof explains. "If we can all do these little things and get our brains trained to do the small things, then our eyes will open up to other things we can do to conserve energy. As a result, it will seem like a natural progression of what we should be doing.

"And if everyone can do just a few little things, I am a firm believer that it will have a huge impact on the health of the planet," she adds.

WHY YOU SHOULD CARE

Energy plays an important role in everyday life. From lighting our homes to fueling our cars and powering our factories, energy is used to make life convenient and efficient—and more fun. Energy is used when we go to the movies, put batteries in our toys, and play arcade games. Energy also helps us improve ways to care for people and help them live longer.

Most of the games that are popular today require electricity or batteries.

Without energy, our world would not look the same. For instance, our homes would be dark and cold. We would not have all the gadgets that make life easier. No one disagrees that energy is an important part of the lifestyle people are used to. But wasting energy can impact our environment at a quicker rate than necessary.

Americans constitute 5 percent of the world's population but consume 25 percent of the world's oil and 23 percent of the coal.[2] As a result, our energy supply is dwindling. Most of the energy our country comes from nonrenewable resources like coal and oil.

When a resource is called nonrenewable, that means it cannot be replaced. Once we use it up, it is gone forever. Nonrenewable resources like oil and coal are also called fossil fuels. Fossil fuels are made from fossilized remains of things that died years ago.

DID YOU KNOW that of the total energy consumed in America, 40 percent is used to generate electricity?[3]

THE FUTURE OF COAL

Coal is formed from giant plants that died in swampy areas many years ago. Over the years, the plants are buried under water and dirt. The heat and pressure from these layers help turn these dead plants into coal. Today, coal is the most plentiful fossil fuel produced in the United States. And the United States has the world's largest known coal reserves. But if we keep using coal at the same rate, it will be gone in about 225 years.[4]

About 92 percent of coal is used to create electricity. Coal is also used to make plastics, fertilizers, and medications. People who mine for coal use giant machines to remove coal from the ground. There are three methods used to get to the coal: surface mining, mountaintop removal mining, and underground mining, which is sometimes called deep mining.

Surface mining is used when the coal is less than two hundred feet underground. Mountaintop removal mining scrapes off the top of a mountain until the coal is visible. Underground mining is used when the coal is buried deep underground; some of these mines are a thousand feet deep.

Mining coal can have a significant impact on the environment. It can destroy land and pollute water near the mine. For this reason, restoring land damaged by surface mining has become part of the mining process.

A coal excavator is used in an underground mine. Coal mining can be harmful to the environment, so we must find ways to develop cleaner energy.

When mining is complete, dirt and rock should be returned to the area. At that point, the land can be used for another purpose.

The coal industry is also working to develop clean coal technologies. These technologies remove coal's sulfur and nitrogen oxide components, which are significant air pollutants.

Because the burning of coal for electricity production is responsible for almost half of all global warming gases released in the atmosphere, experts are urging that we use cleaner forms of energy production.

RESPONSIBLE DRILLING

About 27 percent of the oil used in the United States was imported from other countries and 44 percent of the crude oil processed in refineries was imported.[5] Oil, which is sometimes called petroleum, is formed from the remains of plants and animals covered with layers and layers of mud. The heat and pressure from these layers turns the remains into oil.

Oil is usually found underground in reservoirs. Scientists are able to find oil by studying rock samples and by taking measurements. Some of the tools they use include satellites, sensors, and global positioning devices. These tools allow them to find oil more easily. As a result, when looking for oil, they drill fewer holes than they did in the past.

Drilling for oil can disturb land and ocean habitats and can cause oil spills. Areas disturbed by drilling are sometimes called footprints. Some steps taken to reduce the impact of drilling include using moveable drilling rigs and smaller "slim hole" drilling rigs. As a result, oil-drilling footprints are one-quarter the size of those thirty years ago.[6]

Additionally, with the "rigs to reefs" program, some drilling rigs in the ocean are toppled over and left on the seafloor. They then become artificial reefs that attract fish and other sea life. In six months to one year, the toppled reef is covered with all types of sea creatures including clams, coral, and sponges.

WHERE DID IT ALL BEGIN?

The Industrial Revolution, which occurred between the 1700s and late 1800s, was an exciting time. People were creating machines and equipment that made life easier and more efficient. For instance, steam engines, batteries, and electric-generating power plants were all developed in this time period. Thomas Edison invented the incandescent lightbulb and many other electrical devices during this time. And when an internal combustion engine, which used gasoline, was developed, the age of the automobile was born. During World War I, oil was used to power ships.

All these—electricity, cars, and manufactured goods—allowed people to focus their talents in other areas. For instance, people no longer had to weave their own cloth or make their own clothes. They could go to a store and purchase what they needed. And with cars and trains, they also could get places quicker than ever before.

But all these things require energy, the majority of it from oil and coal. Burning these fossil fuels adds carbon dioxide and other emissions into the atmosphere. Sometimes these emissions are called greenhouse gases because they trap heat in the atmosphere like heat trapped by glass in a greenhouse. Experts say this is making the earth get warmer.

This power plant burns coal to create electricity. This process causes carbon dioxide and other harmful emissions to be given off into the air.

THE EARTH IS FULL OF HOT AIR

Not all greenhouse gases are bad. In fact, gases that occur naturally help regulate the earth's temperature. This natural greenhouse effect allows energy from the sun to be radiated as heat. This helps warm the planet to a temperature where life can survive.

Many scientists say that burning fossil fuels is increasing Earth's natural greenhouse effect. Heat cannot escape into the outer atmosphere, and the earth's temperature rises.

They think deforestation may be contributing too. Deforestation involves cutting down and burning trees. Burning trees releases carbon dioxide into the atmosphere. What's more, cutting down trees means there are fewer trees to absorb carbon dioxide from the atmosphere.

The National Aeronautics and Space Administration (NASA) says that the earth's average temperature has increased by 1.4 degrees Fahrenheit since 1880.[7] What's more, nine of the earth's warmest years have occurred since 2000. The warmest years were 2010 and 2005.

"This decade is warmer than the last decade," says Gavin Schmidt, NASA's Goddard Institute for Space Studies (GISS) climatologist. "The plant is warming [and] the reason it's warming is because we are pumping increasing amounts of carbon dioxide into the atmosphere."[8]

THE DIFFERENCE BETWEEN GLOBAL WARMING AND CLIMATE CHANGE

People often think that *global warming* and *climate change* mean the same thing. They do not. Global warming is an average increase in the temperature of the earth's atmosphere. Both natural and human activities can contribute to global warming. However, when experts talk about global warming, they usually mean warming caused by human activities. Running factories, constructing houses and buildings, and driving cars, trucks, and buses are some of the human activities that can contribute to warming.

Meanwhile, climate change means more than a significant change in temperature. It also takes into account changes in wind and precipitation. According to the National Academy of Sciences, climate change is becoming the preferred term because it communicates that there are other changes taking place besides increasing temperatures.[9]

Changes in climate can have a variety of causes:

- There are changes in the sun's intensity or changes in the earth's orbit around the sun.

Trees absorb carbon dioxide and give off oxygen. People take in oxygen to breathe and give off carbon dioxide. Trees are essential to the life cycle.

- There are changes in the natural processes within the climate system, such as changes in ocean circulation.
- There are human activities that change the atmosphere's makeup, such as burning fossil fuels, deforestation, and urbanization.[10]

Recently, the US government developed a policy to address climate change. Its goals are to slow emissions, strengthen science and technology, and

ALLERGIES AND EMISSIONS

Many people point out that increased carbon dioxide in the atmosphere may enhance plant growth. While this trend might be good for farming, recent research shows that it can worsen respiratory allergies because it can increase pollen in the air. Additionally, scientists have noticed that trees tend to bloom earlier as the climate changes. "We're starting to have what we call 'season creep,'" says Brenda Ekwurzel, a climate scientist with the Union of Concerned Scientists. "Trees are blooming earlier in the spring, and the frost is coming later in the fall, extending the time for allergy sufferers to experience symptoms."[11]

"There's no denying there's a change," adds Paul Ratner, an immunologist with American College of Allergies. "It's definitely bad news for people who have allergies. It doesn't help that warming will also . . . worsen asthma"[12] In fact, the World Health Organization estimates that 235 million people in the world have asthma.[13]

Additionally, researchers have shown that "elevated levels of carbon dioxide stimulate weeds to produce pollen out of proportion with their growth rates . . . and the weediest species seem to thrive . . . in high levels of carbon dioxide."[14] Although scientists are still unable to predict exactly how climate change will affect allergies, recent data suggests that warming will make things worse.[15]

get countries around the world to cooperate more in addressing climate change.

EVERYTHING IS CHANGING

It is no secret that climate change affects people, plants, and animals. For instance, allergies have been linked to changes in climate for years. And diseases like malaria may be sensitive to the climate, too. Recently, scientists have observed other changes as well. These include a rise in sea level, shrinking glaciers, and earlier blooming trees.

Some experts conclude that the strongest evidence of global warming can be found in the Arctic. The Greenland ice sheet is melting at a much faster rate than it was before. If all the ice in the Greenland ice sheet melted, global sea level would rise by about twenty-four feet. Meanwhile, in the last hundred years, sea level in the New York City area has only increased by about one foot.

The problem occurs when storm surges from hurricanes stack on top of this long-term increase. As a result, hurricanes flood places where people are not used to flooding. Hurricane Sandy is an example of this happening. Parts of the New York City subway tunnel system flooded, which was shocking for people. Currently, about a billion people live in areas that would be flooded by a three-foot sea level rise.[16]

"If we are going to do something to mitigate sea-level rise, we need to do it earlier rather than later," says Patrick Applegate, an environmental research associate. "The longer we wait, the more rapidly the changes will take place and the more difficult it will be to change."[17]

Biologist Camille Parmesan estimates that one hundred to two hundred animals that depend on the cold are in deep trouble, including penguins

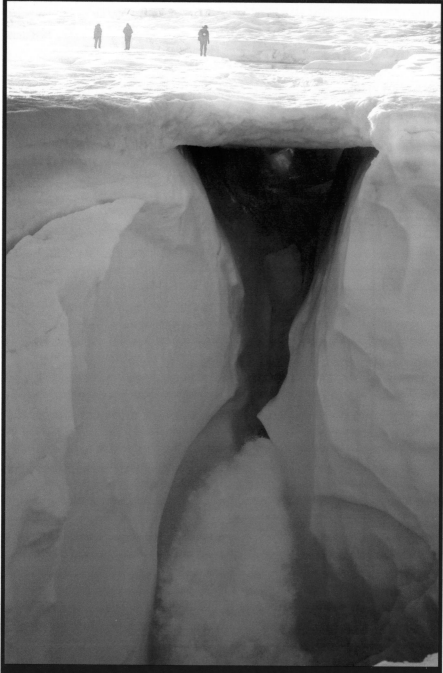

Scientists study the melting Greenland ice sheet, which currently covers 80 percent of the country. Global warming and rising sea levels are significant contributors to the disappearing glaciers.

and polar bears. Cold-dependent species on mountaintops have nowhere to go. "We are . . . seeing species going extinct," she says. "Now we've got the evidence, it's here. It's real. This is not just biologists' intuition. It's what's happening."[18]

According to Douglas Futuyma, a professor of ecology, biologists thought the harmful effects of global warming were further down the road. But they are finding that may not be the case. "I feel as though we are staring crisis in the face," Futuyma says. "It's not just down the road somewhere. It is . . . hurtling toward us. Anyone who is ten years old right now is going to be facing a very different . . . world by the time that they are fifty or sixty."[19]

TAKE ACTION!
LEARN MORE

To learn more about climate change, emissions, and energy use in the United States, commit to following the subject through online news articles or articles in your local newspaper. Keep a notebook of what the experts in this area are doing and predicting.

Draw your own conclusions about the issue. Ask yourself these questions: How important is it that you take action now? What can you do today to affect climate change and improve the environment? What will life be like if you do nothing?

Al Gore poses with his book, *An Inconvenient Truth*. The book and his documentary by the same name started a new discussion in America about global warming.

CHAPTER 2

THINGS ARE GETTING HEATED

GLOBAL WARMING IS A PLANETARY EMERGENCY, according to former Vice President Al Gore. In his documentary, *An Inconvenient Truth,* Gore warns viewers that the earth needs our help or it will change forever.[1]

This documentary, which starred Gore, was a big success. In fact, it was one of the top money-generating documentaries in history, taking in more than $46 million. And the book he wrote to go along with the film was also a hit. It sold millions of copies and even made it to the top of the *New York Times* bestseller list. Gore also won a Nobel Peace Prize and an Academy Award for his film.

But some say that perhaps the film's biggest accomplishment was raising awareness of climate change. Until Gore released his film, there was little attention focused on the issue. Less than one month after the film hit theaters in Australia, a Lowry Institute poll found that global warming was a major concern. In fact, most Australians saw it as a bigger priority than terrorism. Moreover, the poll found that a large portion of Australians wanted something done about climate change—even if it affected the economy.[2]

TRUE OR FALSE?

In the aftermath of the film's success though, some scientists have expressed concerns about the documentary's facts. They argue that some of the main points contain errors or make exaggerated claims. They also worry that Gore may have "gone beyond scientific evidence."[3] Their main concern is not about whether the earth is getting warmer but what will happen if it does. For instance, Dr. Kevin Vranes from the Center for Science and Technology Policy Research at the University of Colorado says that while he is glad Gore "got the message out," he is concerned that he "oversells our certainty about . . . the future."[4]

Gore talks of spikes in temperatures, melting ice caps, rising seas, and dying people. He also points to Hurricane Katrina as one example that storms are going to get larger and more destructive. "Unless we act boldly," he warns, "our world will undergo a string of terrible catastrophes."[5] But others advise caution: "We need to be careful in describing the hurricane story," says Dr. James E. Hansen, an advisor to Gore and director of NASA's Goddard Institute for Space Studies.[6]

Some experts also question the rise in sea level Gore mentions. A report by the United Nations Intergovernmental Panel on Climate Change estimates that the world's seas will rise a maximum of twenty-three inches in this century—down from earlier estimates. Meanwhile, Gore says the seas will rise up to twenty feet. He also portrays New York, Florida, and

Many people believe that climate change will cause more and more major storms like Superstorm Sandy in 2012. That storm caused massive destruction, sending this New Jersey roller coaster into the Atlantic Ocean.

other areas sinking beneath the waves.[7] "Climate change is a real and serious problem. . . . [But] the screaming . . . does not help," says Bjorn Lomborg, a scientist from Denmark. He added that the United Nations panel does not want to scare people. What is needed, he says, is "careful analysis and sound policy."[8]

Meanwhile, there are some special interest groups that do not agree. For instance, Cooler Heads Coalition developed a website designed to "dispel the myths of global warming." Their website states that while global warming is real and carbon dioxide emissions are contributing to it, it is not a crisis. "Global warming in the 21st century is likely to be modest, and the net impacts may well be beneficial in some places," they say. "Even in the worst case, humanity will be much better off in 2100 than it is today."[9] The coalition notes that death rates related to extreme weather have declined by more than 98 percent since 1920. As far as the future goes, the coalition says that rising sea levels in the twenty-first century will be measured in inches rather than feet.[10]

Due to mounting evidence, groups like Cooler Heads are in the minority. There is no question that global warming is a reality. How we react to the situation is what will make a difference in the future. Richard C. J. Sommerville, a climate modeler and author of *The Forgiving Air: Understanding Environmental Change,* says the American people should be concerned about climate change.

> "Concerned" is a good word for climate change. Not alarmed, and not [indifferent]. So far as we know, this is a phenomenon with a long time scale. On the other hand, we have to keep in mind that there have been surprises in the past. The ozone hole is a wonderful example. There was a theory that ozone would be slowly depleted if our use of ozone-depleting chemicals such as air conditioning refrigerants was not drastically reduced. Indeed, the discovery that half the ozone over the Antarctic atmosphere disappeared every southern spring was a huge surprise. The Montreal protocol resulted in a shift towards more environmentally benign chemicals, and the hope is that the ozone hole will restore itself in the next few decades. And there's a lot of recent evidence that the climate system is capable of behaving like a switch rather than a dial, and producing surprises.[11]

POWER SURGE

The concern over climate change has resulted in a global focus on finding new ways to provide energy. Resources like the sun, wind, water, and waste products are being investigated because they are renewable. If an energy resource can be replaced, that means it is renewable. Unlike oil and coal, renewable energy will not run out and it is better for the environment because it does not cause pollution or damage the earth. For this reason, renewable energy is also called clean energy or green power.

The Environmental Protection Agency (EPA) says green power is energy "that provides the highest environmental benefit." In other words, electricity is considered green when it can be produced with no human-caused greenhouse gas emissions. On the other hand, the EPA does not consider

These turbines convert wind into energy. Wind power is one type of renewable resource that could lessen our dependence on fossil fuels.

nuclear power a source of green power because it requires mining and long-term storage of radioactive waste.[12]

///

THE KYOTO PROTOCOL

Despite the disagreements over global warming, the scientific consensus has resulted in nations recognizing that something must be done to address energy use and emissions. As a result, an agreement was reached by the United Nations Conference on Climate Change in Kyoto, Japan, in 1997.

The agreement is known as the Kyoto Protocol, and it went into effect February 16, 2005. A total of 141 countries accepted and signed the treaty—but not the United States, Australia, or Monaco. Through the agreement, major industrial nations pledged to reduce their emissions of greenhouse gases between 2008 and 2012. Even though China and India, the world's largest polluters, signed the treaty, they did not have to address emissions until after 2012 because they were considered developing countries.

The American delegation signed the protocol in 1997, but the Senate has refused to ratify the treaty. They feel the targeted reductions are so strict that it would have a big economic impact on the country.[13]

///

SOLAR ENERGY

Perhaps one of the most powerful forms of renewable energy is solar power, or power from the sun. In fact, just one hour of sunlight has enough power to meet world energy demand for a year.[14] Solar power can be used to provide heat and make electricity. When it is used as a heat source, water and air in buildings and homes are heated by using solar panels on the roof.

A solar-powered calculator is a common example of using power from the sun to operate something. But getting energy from the sun is expensive and inefficient (we can only convert 10 percent of incoming solar radiation into useful energy such as electricity). Experts are still trying to find cost-effective ways to use energy from the sun.

DID YOU KNOW that the average person is responsible for emitting ninety-four pounds of carbon dioxide every day? As a result, it takes four trees, which act like air filters, to offset the carbon dioxide each person creates in a month.[15]

The solar panels on this house will convert energy from the sun to help provide heat and electricity.

WIND ENERGY

Using the wind to make electricity is not a new idea. Windmills, which are often found on farms, are examples that have been around for a long time. But this type of windmill can make only a small amount of electricity. As a result, power companies are building what is called a wind farm to harvest wind. A wind farm has lots of huge wind turbines. These turbines are built on flat, open areas where the wind blows at least fourteen miles per hour or offshore in the ocean where wind blows almost constantly.

When the wind turns the blades of a windmill, it spins a turbine inside a generator to produce electricity. Currently, wind farms produce enough electricity to meet the needs of more than six hundred thousand families in the United States. Hawaii has the largest wind turbine in the world. It is twenty stories tall and its blades are as long as a football field.[16]

BIOMASS ENERGY

The word *biomass* means natural material and includes materials like wood, paper, sludge, and other organic waste products. Places that contain a lot of biomass, such as farms and landfills, have become significant producers of biomass power. Nearly half of the renewable energy in the United States comes from biomass. In fact, biomass power provides enough electricity for two million homes.[17]

Burning biomass used to be the most common way to capture energy. But research has shown that now there are more efficient and cleaner ways to use biomass. For instance, it can be converted into liquid fuel by cooking it using a process called gasification to produce combustible gases.

In Iowa, one company recycles more than 150 tons of biomass material every day to create electricity for four thousand homes. The biomass they use includes leftover wood, cornstalks and corncobs, and paper and cardboard that cannot be recycled in other ways. Meanwhile, in Wisconsin people are using their local trash dump to create energy. As the trash breaks down, or decomposes, it gives off a gas called methane. A machine captures the methane and uses it to produce electricity. A similar process can be used to turn the methane gas from animal waste or cow manure into electricity. The EPA has helped convert 360 landfills into energy producers. In landfills, microorganisms break down organic materials into methane, which is converted into electricity using generators.

DID YOU KNOW that anything that does work uses energy? For example, playing soccer, growing a tomato plant and listening to music on your phone all require energy. What's more, energy comes in many different forms and can be turned into different forms and stored.

WATER-GENERATED ENERGY

Around the world, hydropower or waterpower is the most commonly used renewable energy resource. In fact, hydropower provides enough power for 28 million people. And it has been around for a while.[18]

The first hydroelectric power plant opened in the United States in 1882. By the 1940s nearly half of the country's electricity came from hydropower. But after World War II, coal power plants became more popular.

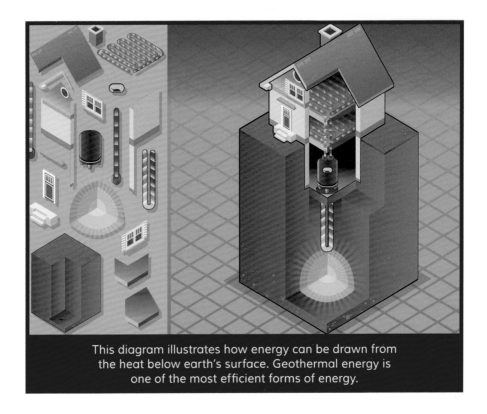

This diagram illustrates how energy can be drawn from the heat below earth's surface. Geothermal energy is one of the most efficient forms of energy.

Today, hydropower provides about 10 percent of the electricity in the United States, which is equivalent to 500 million barrels of oil. Most of the country's hydroelectric power plants are in California, Oregon, and Washington. The Grand Coulee Dam in Washington is the biggest hydroelectric dam in the United States. Construction on this dam began in 1933 and was not finished until 1942. Today, it is the largest hydropower producer in the United States. It generates enough electricity to power 2.3 million households per year.[19]

GEOTHERMAL ENERGY

Geothermal power is found under the earth. Volcanoes and geysers are examples of geothermal power. The lava and steam that are emitted by volcanoes and geysers come from underground heat. To use geothermal power, pipes are buried more than four feet underground. These pipes carry liquid that absorbs the heat and brings it back to the surface to heat buildings. In the summer, the system works in reverse by absorbing heat in the building or home and moving it back into the earth. Geothermal heating is very energy-efficient because almost no energy is wasted.

Geothermal power can also be used to make electricity. A power plant taps into the steam or hot water underground to produce electricity. The world's largest complex of geothermal power plants is The Geysers in California. It produces enough electricity for more than 725,000 homes or a city the size of San Francisco.[20]

Addressing the problems in our environment involves using renewable energy. But that is not the only answer. We also need to conserve non-renewable energy by building and using more energy-efficient houses, communities, products, and cars.

CAP THE CARBON

Some experts believe that one way to encourage people to conserve energy and address climate change is to charge businesses for carbon emissions. Businesses may be more motivated to use renewable energy when they are charged for polluting the environment.[21]

One way to do this is through a cap-and-trade system. This system puts a cap, or limit, on how much carbon a company can produce. Meanwhile, companies that produce less carbon than allowed can sell credits to those who are over the limit.

The Chicago Climate Exchange (CCX) was developed based on this idea. The CCX, which was the world's first carbon market, functioned like the stock market except that emission rights were traded instead of stock. It traded greenhouse gas allowances between 2003 and 2010 but has since disbanded.

Participating companies were required to reduce emissions by 6 percent between 2000 and 2010. If a company reduced emissions more than that, they could sell their extra credits on the market. In turn, companies that could not make the necessary reductions could buy someone else's excess.

The belief behind the cap-and-trade system is that carbon levels will fall. Greener companies can make money. And people will invest in renewable energy.[22]

As a result of their efforts, CCX says its 450 members achieved reductions of 700 million tons of greenhouse gas emissions over the seven-year life of the cap-and-trade program. Eighty-eight percent of those emissions were through direct industrial emission cuts and 12 percent through offsetting.[23]

WATCH YOUR WASTE

There is no denying that the world's easily available supply of oil and coal is decreasing and renewable energy promises to reduce our dependence on fossil fuels and reduce global warming emissions at the same time. But most experts agree that the best way to address the world's dwindling supply of fossil fuels is to become more efficient with what we use.

For instance, in 2012 Americans generated about 251 million tons of trash and recycled and composted almost 87 million tons of this material. This is equivalent to a 34.5 percent recycling rate. On average, this means people recycled or composted less than two pounds of their individual waste generation, which is 4.38 pounds per person per day.[24]

Waste is processed in a recycling factory. While it may seem that recycling has become widespread, Americans still throw away huge amounts of trash.

Experts say that America has wasted energy for years.[25] However, now that prices are going up, people are looking for ways to save energy—and money. They have found that renewable energy not only can save them money, but can also help the environment. According to McKinsey Global Institute (MGI), we could cut the world's energy demand in half by 2020 by cutting waste in simple ways such as turning off lights in office buildings at night. MGI also says that if companies spend $170 billion to make improvements like green buildings and cars that get better mileage, that could create $900 billion per year in savings by 2020.[26]

Finally, experts agree that conserving energy will buy us the time we need to perfect renewable energy sources and make them more affordable. Ultimately, the long-term goal is that green energy will replace fossil fuels as our primary energy source. "The biggest source of immediately available 'new' energy is the energy that we waste every day," says Samuel Bodman, former US Department of Energy secretary.[27]

TAKE ACTION!
CONSERVE ENERGY

Most of the energy you use at home comes from burning fossil fuels. When you choose to use less energy, this means burning fewer fossil fuels and putting less carbon dioxide into the atmosphere.

Challenge your family to cut your household's energy use by 10 percent. Start by conducting an energy audit to see where you are using the most energy. You can visit energy.gov to learn more. Then, keep track of your progress by comparing your gas and electric bills from previous years.

Here are ideas on how to use less energy. See if you can come up with three additional ways to reduce energy use in your home.

Unplug your devices. Be sure to unplug video game consoles, cell phone chargers, tablets and computers whenever you can. Or consider buying a smart power strip, which automatically cuts off power when you turn off an appliance.

Make smart purchases. Look at the label when shopping for appliances, televisions, computers and other devices. Energy-efficient appliances and electronics typically use between 10 and 50 percent less energy than regular models.

Discuss switching to green power. Talk with your family about switching to renewable energy. You can explore your options at the Green Power Network's website under the link "Buying Green Power" (apps3.eere.energy.gov/greenpower/buying/index.shtml)

CHAPTER 3

HOME IS WHERE THE GREEN IS

JUST OUTSIDE OF COLUMBUS, OHIO, CRAIG AND AMANDA Pickerill built their dream home—a green home, to be exact. This 3,900-square-foot structure was the first of its kind in the area and offers the Pickerills energy-efficient living at its best. When building, they had three principles in mind, including energy efficiency, clean air, and renewable materials. "For instance, all the wood we trimmed with was cut down thirty years ago. So we didn't cut down any trees to [build our home]," Pickerill says. "I found a lady whose father had cut the wood out of Hocking Hills in the '70s and he just had it stored in his barn since then. We then went and had it milled at a local mill."[1]

They also wanted to avoid using materials that give off harmful gases. Many products give off gas when they are new, Pickerill says. This released gas is actually chemicals used in making the materials. This process is called off-gassing. "We have no carpet in our house and we have no vinyl in our home," he explains. "Vinyl is soft and it off-gases for years. It's

People everywhere are building more green (also called "eco") homes. This one in Denmark includes wood floors and energy-saving devices, and the dome shape reduces amount of materials used.

just like when you get a new car. That new car smell is off-gassing of all the chemicals."

To achieve energy efficiency, Pickerill says they built an Energy Star home. Energy Star house certification is based on an energy review of the home during the building process. A company reviews the home's systems and building materials to determine the rating. "We received Energy Star's Five Star Plus rating, which is the highest rating possible," he says. "Our house is about twice as energy efficient as the typical new-build house."

The Pickerills estimate that they save about $150 per month on their heating bills. And their gas bill is only fifteen dollars per month. The savings they are experiencing are more than the US Department of Energy (DOE) estimates. The DOE says that building energy-efficient homes has saved homeowners an average of four hundred dollars per year. Meanwhile, the extra construction costs have been as little as five hundred dollars more to build an energy-efficient home.[2]

Craig Pickerill believes that a great deal of their savings is due to the type of systems they chose for their home. For instance, their water heater is efficient because it is an on-demand system. "It only heats water when you need it," he explains. "I think the water heater is about 30 percent of the electric bill [in traditional homes]. So it saves a lot of money."

The Pickerills also have a dual-source heat pump, which helps save money, too. A heat pump transfers heat from the outside air to warm the home rather than creating it using fuel. During milder winters, it costs less to heat a house with a heat pump than with a furnace that burns fossil fuels. Using a heat pump is efficient until the outside temperature gets too cold. Then the systems become inefficient, Pickerill says. At that point, it allows the gas furnace to take over. "I think at around 20 degrees, heat pumps begin to cost more to run," he says. "That's when our heater switches over to gas heat. So dual-source means that we use a heat pump at warmer temperatures and gas heat when it becomes colder."

To achieve the goal of clean air and increase energy efficiency, Pickerill says they concentrated on "sealing the envelope" of their home. "When you seal the envelope of your home, you want to have such good insulation that your house can't really breathe," he says. "Then, you use a heat exchanger, which brings outside air in and exchanges it with inside air." Heat exchangers also help with the heating and cooling process. For instance, the exchanger takes the warmth out of the air you are blowing out and puts it into the cooler air that is coming in.

The overall structure of the Pickerills' home also makes it greener and helps them use less energy. For example, their home is better insulated than traditional homes—even in the basement. Pickerill explains:

> We used the Colorado Green Building Checklist to build our
> house. I chose it because it is a point system that made it
> really simple. For instance you get more points if you choose
> a high level insulation system. So we built our home using
> structural insulated panels. Those are called SIPs and it is
> a really easy way to build an energy-efficient home.

SIPs have an outside wall made of concrete. Meanwhile, the middle of the wall is continuous foam insulation. Pickerill compares the assembly of the walls to that of "putting a kid's toy together." The challenge, he says, is finding a builder who is comfortable with the construction. "It is hard to find people to build your home. They are not comfortable building with these new systems," he says. "They have been building

This builder is holding a section of SIP (structural insulated panel) as he works on an energy-efficient home in Atlanta. The insulation helps make the home weather-tight, reducing energy use.

houses out of wood, or stick and frame homes, for their whole careers. When you tell them you want to build out of these other things, they think you are crazy."

Their basement is also unlike those found in traditional homes. Rather than having it made out of poured concrete or block, their basement was made in a factory with insulation built into it. It took a crane to install it. "Concrete is a really poor insulator," Pickerill says. "You lose a lot of heat through your basement."

Finally, the Pickerills have long-term plans to use renewable energy to heat their home. "We put a standing seam metal roof on our house and conduit all the way to the attic from the basement. The rear of our house faces south too," he says. "Our plan is to add solar panels in the next year."

ENERGY STAR RATING

Energy Star is a symbol used for energy efficiency. For this logo to appear on products, they must meet standards set by the US Department of Energy and the Environmental Protection Agency.

The goal of the Energy Star program, which was developed in 1992, is to reduce both pollution and energy bills. Energy Star products include refrigerators, dishwashers, clothes washers, lights, and so on. For instance, Energy Star washers use thirteen gallons of water per load compared to the twenty-three gallons used by a standard machine. That's a savings of more than three thousand gallons of water per year.

The Energy Star label on this washing machine tells the buyer that the product meets government standards for energy efficiency.

What's more, if your washer is more than ten years old, it is using more water than it needs to. Experts estimate that there are billion top-loading washers in the United States. Twenty-five million of those washers are at least ten years old and still in use across the country.

Washers built before 2003 are significantly less efficient than newer models. These inefficient washers cost consumers $2.9 billion each year in energy and water. As a result, if you have a standard clothes washer that is more than ten years old, it's costing you on average $180 a year.

If every clothes washer purchased in the United States was Energy Star certified, we could save more than $4 billion each year and prevent more than 19 billion pounds of annual greenhouse gas emissions, equal to the emissions from 1.8 million vehicles.[3]

BUILDING GREEN

Building a new home is exciting. From fresh paint and new flooring to a new design and location, people enjoy seeing a home come together. However, building a new home can be hard on the environment. For this reason, more and more people are looking into ways to build greener homes. "Green homes are definitely on the radar screens of consumers," says Christine Ervin, CEO of the Green Building Council. "Within . . . years, many more people will be aware of the comfort and affordability of green homes."[4]

The main idea behind the green home building movement is to use resources efficiently. This means not only using renewable energy like solar, wind, and geothermal power but also choosing materials that do little, if any, harm to the environment. An example might include using reclaimed or salvaged lumber rather than fresh lumber to build walls and support beams. There are some companies that specialize in getting building materials from older homes that are about to be torn down. Instead of discarding the materials, this lumber can be put back into new construction.

Other ways to make sure resources are used efficiently and new home construction is as green as possible include:

- Making sure the home does not use a lot of energy—this can be done with everything from using efficient appliances to incorporating renewable energy like solar power into the design.
- Using recycled and responsibly harvested materials with fewer chemicals (for instance, a bamboo floor is much easier on the environment than a vinyl floor).

- Creating cleaner, more breathable air—aside from using equipment to ensure the air quality is top-notch, certain materials like paint and flooring also impact air quality.

- Making sure the impact on land and water is as low as possible—for instance there are lots of ways to minimize the use of water in the home including everything from collecting rainwater to controlling the energy used to heat water.[5]

Building greener homes is catching on. Home builders say that increasing energy costs, consumer demand for green homes, and the better performance of green products are driving the green building movement. In fact, 82 percent of builders say energy efficiency tops the list of green methods requested.[6]

BUILDING ENERGY FREE

A Zero Energy Home (ZEH) combines energy-efficient construction and appliances with renewable energy systems, such as solar power. The result is a home that produces its own energy and sometimes more energy than it needs. Even though the home might be connected to a utility grid, it uses net zero energy.[7]

One benefit of a ZEH is that the home's construction reduces temperature fluctuations. It also increases reliability because it can be designed to work even during blackouts. Finally, a ZEH saves energy and reduces pollution.

The US Department of Energy has partnered with building professionals and organizations to further develop the ZEH concept. To date, only a few of these homes have been constructed and researched.

The potential for the green building movement is huge. In fact, it is expected that about 1.5 million new homes will be built and furnished each year. Just how many of those new homes will be built green is uncertain. But experts are optimistic. "All homes will one day be green," predicts David Johnston, author of *Building Green in a Black and White World*. "It makes too much sense for it not to happen."

HOME GREEN HOME

Experts expect to see more people like the Pickerills making their dream homes green. They also anticipate that in the coming years, small-scale renewable energy projects such as installing solar panels on the roof or purchasing small wind turbines are going to become increasingly popular.

But for people who cannot afford to build a new home or remodel an existing one, there are other options. For instance, some homeowners are able to buy green power directly from an electricity provider. More than 850 regulated utilities spanning nearly every state offer green pricing programs. The term *green pricing* refers to an optional utility service. This service allows customers to support a greater investment in renewable energy by paying a premium on their electric bill. This fee covers any above-market costs of acquiring renewable energy resources.[8]

Many states implemented electricity competition, which makes purchasing green power even easier. Under electricity competition, consumers can choose who they buy their electricity from. As a result, they have the freedom to choose a provider that emphasizes a commitment to renewable energy.

According to the DOE, "by choosing to purchase a green power product, you can support increased development of renewable energy sources."[9]

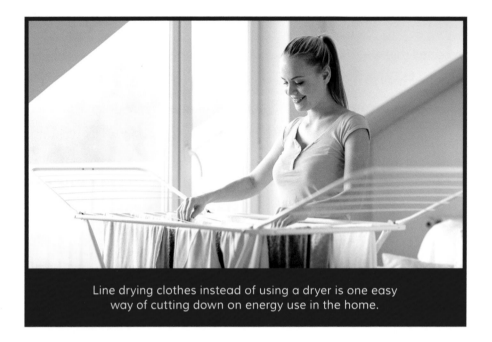

Line drying clothes instead of using a dryer is one easy way of cutting down on energy use in the home.

This support then reduces the burning of fossil fuels, such as coal and oil. The DOE website lists organizations that offer green power.

Finally, before taking on a huge remodeling project or hoisting a wind turbine in the yard, experts recommend people look first at conserving energy and using energy more efficiently. Energy conservation involves changing behavior, like air-drying clothes instead of using a clothes dryer. Energy efficiency involves using less energy to do the same thing, like installing a more energy-efficient lightbulb to light a room. Therefore, if you want to help preserve the environment and save money, it makes good sense to do all of the reasonable conservation and efficiency measures first.

After all, most people use more energy at home than anyplace else. Energy is used to heat and cool the house, to heat water for cleaning and bathing, and to power electronic devices such as televisions, DVD players, and computers.

//

GREEN HOME INSPIRATION

The Smart Home featured at the Chicago Museum of Science and Industry is an example of a green home. Featuring everything from a recycled plastic deck to bathroom tiles made out of recycled wine bottles, the 2,500-square-foot (232-square-meter) home is an example of environmentally responsible living. The home, which shows visitors how easy it is to be green, also includes a solar paneled roof and 300-gallon barrels to collect rainwater.

"We tried to look for ideas in every choice that we make in our homes . . . hoping that everyone who goes through it will be inspired to make some change on some level," says Michelle Kaufmann, the architect who designed the Smart Home.[10]

Museum officials say the goal of the exhibit is to show people that everyone can save energy and conserve resources—"whether it is an entire house or a single feature."[11]

"One thing that is fundamental to green building is that it can look like anything," says David Johnston, who owns an international green building consulting firm in Colorado. "It can be a regular Craftsman house or a Cape Cod house . . . or an adobe house in Santa Fe. You don't have to change what the home looks like to make it green."[12]

//

SLAYING ENERGY VAMPIRES

Some electronics use power even when they are turned off. These items are called energy vampires. For instance, a cell phone charger that is left plugged in is still sucking in small amounts of energy even though it is not charging anything. Other vampires include televisions, computers, and printers. Even your electric toothbrush is an energy vampire. It is using energy just by being plugged in.

Although the energy cell phone chargers and electric toothbrushes are using may seem small, when all the wasted energy is added up, it equals about $3 billion a year in the United States alone. For instance, gaming stations can eat up thirty-two dollars a year and the computer accounts for another thirty-four dollars. And that plasma TV is sucking down sixteen dollars a year even while it is turned off.[13]

TAKE ACTION!
SLAY YOUR VAMPIRES

To slay the energy vampires in your home, consider unplugging the following items:

- hand-held vacuums
- DVD players
- televisions
- power drills and electric screwdrivers
- chargers for cell phones, tablets and other devices
- VCRs
- automatic coffeemakers
- empty appliances
- computers and printers

Another option is to purchase a power strip and plug everything into the strip. Then all you have to do is flip a switch and the power is cut off. Craig Pickerill says another option is a smart outlet.

"It completely turns your television off when it's not on," he says. "There are lots of things people can do to save energy. You don't have to build a new house to cut down on your energy use."

Experts agree that slaying energy vampires is one of the easiest ways to conserve energy and protect the environment. Plus, it can save you money each month on your electric bill.

Don't leave your charger plugged in when it's not in use! It will continue to use energy.

HOW BIG IS YOUR FOOTPRINT?

Your carbon footprint is determined by adding up the amount of carbon dioxide produced from all your activities. Transportation, time spent using electronics, where you eat, and what you eat are all considered. For example, when you use a carbon footprint calculator you would answer questions about how you get to school, where you eat most of your meals, and how you spend your time.

Carbon footprints are used to measure one's impact on the environment. Having a small carbon footprint is better than being Bigfoot. Unfortunately, most Americans have big feet when it comes to carbon footprints. In fact, on average, each person in the United States is responsible for about twenty-two tons of carbon dioxide emissions every year, according to statistics compiled by the United Nations. That is far bigger than the world average of six tons.[14]

The best way to reduce the size of your carbon footprint is to use less energy.

DID YOU KNOW that across the United States home refrigerators use the electricity of twenty-five large power plants every year?[15]

OFFSETTING CARBON USE

The idea behind carbon offsets is that you reduce the amount of carbon dioxide you put into the environment by offsetting the carbon emissions you cannot reduce on your own. What this means is that once you have conserved energy and cut back as much as you can, you then pay a group like CarbonFund or TerraPass to help reduce the size of your carbon footprint. These companies invest in projects like developing renewable energy, improving energy efficiency, and implementing tree-planting projects.

Each year, Christy Radanof and her family contribute to an organization that plants trees across the country. "[We do this to] offset our carbon emissions for our vehicles. It costs us about $35 a year to take care of both of our cars."[16]

However, there is some disagreement over the accuracy of carbon offsets. For instance, some experts argue that projects taken on by companies offering carbon offsets do not really compensate for the carbon the person is releasing into the air.[17]

"It is very unproductive to leave people with the impression that we could possibly plant our way out of the problem," says Joe Romm, an expert on carbon offsets.[18]

GREEN LAWS, PLANS AND AGREEMENTS

The United States is realizing how important it is to conserve energy and become more energy efficient. In December 2007, President George W. Bush signed a law that requires automakers to develop more fuel-efficient cars. It also called for improved energy efficiency in refrigerators, freezers, dishwashers, and even lightbulbs. In fact, the law states that lightbulbs will need to become 70 percent more efficient. "I firmly believe this country needs to have a comprehensive energy strategy," said President Bush.[19]

The law focuses on energy conservation on everything from "lightbulbs to light trucks," said Representative John Dingell of Michigan. The new lighting standards alone will lower annual electricity bills by $13 billion in 2020, remove the need for sixty midsize power plants, and reduce emissions by 100 million tons a year, says the Alliance to Save Energy.[20]

In June 2014, the EPA proposed the Clean Power Plan. It is the first-ever carbon pollution standards for existing power plants. Power plants are the largest single source of carbon pollution. They account for about one-third of all domestic greenhouse gas emissions. Under the plan, experts predict it will put the country on a path toward a 30 percent reduction in carbon pollution by 2030.[21]

In November 2014, President Barack Obama and Chinese leaders laid out a plan to reduce greenhouse gas emissions. The announcement was a historic step because the world's two largest economies, energy consumers, and carbon emitters were able to come together and demonstrate leadership on an issue that impacts the entire world.[22] In the United States, the goal is to reduce greenhouse gas emissions between 26 and

Recent administrations have passed laws in an effort to encourage energy conservation. Here, President Obama signs the Energy Efficiency Improvement Act of 2015.

28 percent below 2005 levels by 2025. Meanwhile, China announced its intent to peak carbon emissions around 2030.[23]

LIVING LEAN AND GREEN

Because so much of our world revolves around energy, we are confronted with lifestyle decisions that affect our environment every day. And the choices we make can impact the quality of life for those who follow us. We use energy in almost every aspect of our lives. It is used in making and transporting goods. And it is used when we get rid of things we no longer need.

One of the biggest choices any of us will make is how we will live each day. For instance, will we live any way we want, not consider the impact it has on the world? Or will we consider our purchases and how we dispose of our waste?

Almost everyone is familiar with the three Rs—reduce, reuse, and recycle. In fact, the phrase has been used so much that it is now commonplace. But even though the message has been around awhile, it still applies. The three Rs are the key to saving energy and living a greener lifestyle. They include:

- **Reduce waste.** This is done by making smart decisions when purchasing products, including trying to buy products without a lot of extra packaging. It also involves buying things that have been made from recycled products.
- **Reuse materials.** This involves looking for creative ways to reuse containers and products rather than pitching them in the trash can.
- **Recycle.** Lots of things can be recycled—everything from paper and plastic to food scraps, yard trimmings, and electronics. Recycling can also involve selling or giving away used clothing and furniture instead of dumping them in the garbage.

TAKE ACTION!
REDUCE, REUSE AND RECYCLE

- Save at least 2,400 pounds (1,089 kilograms) of carbon dioxide a year by recycling at least half of your household waste.
- Save 1,200 pounds (544 kilograms) of carbon dioxide by avoiding heavily packaged products and cutting down your garbage by 10 percent.
- Reduce your use of fertilizers and water by creating homemade compost and using it on your yard.[24]

The world is becoming more aware of the need for energy conservation and protecting the environment. As a result, it is getting easier to incorporate the three Rs into everyday life. For instance, products made from recycled material are becoming increasingly popular and are easier to find in the marketplace.

EATING LEAN AND GREEN

Most of us probably do not think about where our food came from when we sit down to eat. But where and how our food is grown can make a difference on the environment. Energy is used to grow, transport, package, and cook our food. What's more, some production methods pump more carbon dioxide into the environment than others. In order to eat green, a lot of factors must be considered.

For instance, eating locally produced foods is typically easier on the environment. But not always, warn some experts. Food miles (the distance your food is transported to get to you) are a great indicator of localness but not of environmental impact.[25] In other words, local food can be best if it is purchased in season. So, purchasing a locally grown watermelon in central Michigan in the middle of winter, when it is not in season, may actually require more energy than purchasing it someplace else. Growing the watermelon locally might take more energy than it takes to transport it from a warmer climate. In the middle of winter, energy would be needed to heat, light, and irrigate a greenhouse. "You can't just look at the transportation piece," says Gail Feenstra, a food analyst at the University of California. "It's one piece of the whole puzzle."[26]

How food is grown and harvested also plays a role. For instance, some experts say that "New York state apples can be less eco-friendly than those

DID YOU KNOW that every time you open the refrigerator door, up to 30 percent of the cold air can escape?[27]

imported from New Zealand, where growing conditions produce greater yields with less energy."[28]

According to the organization Living Green, there are a number of benefits of eating green:

- The average American dinner travels 1,500 miles (2,414 kilometers) before reaching the dinner plate. Eating local food can reduce the consumption of fossil fuels and wasteful packing materials.
- Buying locally keeps money in your community.

Farmers markets like the one shown here are ideal places to find locally grown food that is in-season.

- Local farmers' markets, which sell items that are grown in season, reduce the amount of energy required to grow and transport the food to you by one-fifth.

- Buying organic can be beneficial because soils capture and store carbon dioxide at much higher levels than soils from conventional farms.

DID YOU KNOW companies that make new products from recycled materials use 30 percent less energy?[29]

WATCH OUT FOR GREENWASHING

More and more people are going green. Consequently, some companies are trying to cash in on this movement by using a tactic known as greenwashing. Greenwashing is based on the term *whitewashing*. When someone whitewashes something, he is trying to make it seem more innocent than it really is. With greenwashing, a company spends more time and money claiming to be green than actually becoming green.

An example of greenwashing is the hotel chain that claims to be green because it encourages guests to reuse towels and sheets rather than having them changed every day. But that is all the chain is doing. While reusing towels does save water, there is much more the company could be doing. In other areas of their business, they are doing little to save water and energy.

In 2007, TerraChoice, a science-based marketing firm, focused attention on greenwashing with a study known as The Six Sins of Greenwashing. Their study found that 99 percent of the more than one thousand products they reviewed were guilty of greenwashing.[30]

Since then, TerraChoice has joined the Underwriters Laboratories Environment and a seventh Sin has been added.[31]

The Seven Sins of greenwashing include:

1. **Sin of the Hidden Trade-Off:** An example would be "energy-efficient" electronics that contain hazardous materials. Fifty-seven percent of all environmental claims committed this sin.

2. **Sin of No Proof:** An example would be shampoos claiming to be "certified organic" but with no verifiable certification. Twenty-six percent of environmental claims committed this sin.

3. **Sin of Vagueness:** Examples include products claiming to be 100 percent natural when many naturally occurring substances are hazardous, like arsenic and formaldehyde. This sin was seen in 11 percent of environmental claims.

4. **Sin of Irrelevance:** Examples include products claiming to be CFC-free even though CFCs were banned twenty years ago. CFCs, or chlorofluorocarbons, are compounds that contribute to the depletion of the ozone layer. This sin was seen in 4 percent of environmental claims.

5. **Sin of Fibbing:** Examples include products falsely claiming to be certified by an internationally recognized environmental standard like EcoLogo, Energy Star, or Green Seal. This sin was found in less than one percent of environmental claims.

6. **Sin of Lesser of Two Evils:** An example would be organic cigarettes or "environmentally friendly" pesticides. This sin occurred in one percent of environmental claims.

7. **Sin of Worshiping False Labels:** When marketers create a false suggestion or a certification-like image to mislead consumers into thinking that a product has been through a legitimate green certification process. One

example of this Sin is a brand of aluminum foil with certi-fication-like images that show the name of the company's own in-house environmental program for which there is no explanation.[32]

The goal of the studies is to help shoppers find the truth. Most of the time, the claims made about products were not actual lies, but they were misleading to the average consumer. For instance, some garbage bags that are sold are labeled compostable. What this state-ment implies is that a person can throw the bags into a compost bin or a landfill and the bags will break down quickly. However, plastic bags like these still take years to break down—unless they are sent to an institutional compost-ing facility. Once at the facility, the bags must be stirred with huge tractors to create heat and speed the breakdown process. But most consumers do not know this is what is meant by compostable. They read the label and believe the bags will turn into dirt without any intervention.

Having a label like this one does not guarantee that a product is actually organic. It may be a case of greenwashing.

"Consumers are inundated with products [like this] that make green claims," McDougall says. "Some are accurate, certified and verifiable, while others are just plain fibbing to sell products."[33]

TAKE ACTION!

WALKING THE WALK

Your parents do not have to build a new home, and they don't have to take on a large remodeling project to conserve energy. There are a number of things that can be done around the house that will save energy—and money. Aside from shutting off lights, getting rid of energy vampires, lowering the thermostat, and replacing lightbulbs, here are some other ideas:

- Ask your parents if you can put a plastic bottle filled with water or pennies in the toilet tank. The weight of the water bottle will cause the tank to use less water every time you flush. In fact, *Plenty* magazine estimates that it will save about a quart to half a gallon per flush.[34]

- Make sure the lint filter on your clothes dryer is clean. The dryer becomes more energy efficient and runs better without lint clogging it.

- Reuse batteries when you can. You can stretch the life of your batteries if you switch them before you pitch them. For instance, batteries that no longer power a flashlight might still work in a television remote.

- Turn off dripping faucets every time you see them. One drop per second can add up to 165 gallons (625 liters) of water a month—that is more water than one person uses in two weeks.[35]

Cars give off pollutants and use a lot of energy.
Carpooling or taking public transportation are good
ways to reduce the number of cars on the road.

CHAPTER 4

DRIVING GREEN

WHILE THE KIRK FAMILY FROM WYLIE, TEXAS, MAY not own a hybrid vehicle, they still do what they can to avoid pumping carbon dioxide into the air. To conserve energy, they only own one car. They also carpool, combine errands into one trip, and encourage their daughter, Katie, to bike to school.

"Sometimes it is inconvenient trying to conserve gasoline," admits Jennifer Kirk, who moved from Ohio to Texas several years ago with her husband, Matt, and daughter, Katie. "But we try hard not to go driving around unless we have multiple things to do. For example, I'll delay grocery shopping until I have to go to the bank across the street too."[1]

Kirk, who is a prekindergarten teacher and full-time college student, is creative when it comes to conserving gasoline. Aside from trying to schedule her college courses to correspond with her carpool buddy, she also looks for ways to combine errands with her friends and family. "When there were sales for teachers at the office supply stores, a bunch of us got together to go all at once," says Kirk. "[My husband] Matt and I also do our errands together instead of separately."

And although the Kirks do not own a hybrid car, they looked into them when they purchased their Ford Escape in 2006. "We looked at hybrids when we bought our last car, but for the size we need they are too expensive," Kirk said. "They are great if you don't travel seventeen hours to Ohio twice a year [to visit family]! We only own one car. So it is important our family fit in it with all our stuff."

Hybrids have changed a lot since the Kirks purchased their car in 2006. By the end of 2010, the number of hybrids available grew to twenty-nine different models. And they have grown in popularity.[2] As of October 2014, three million hybrid trucks and cars have been sold in the United States. Considering that the market started out with only seventeen hybrids sold in 1999, this is a large gain in such a short time.[3]

PLUGGED INTO REDUCING EMISSIONS

Some experts believe that emission-free electric cars are the wave of the future. These all-electric vehicles (EVs) run on electricity only. They are propelled by one or more electric motors that are powered by rechargeable battery packs. EVs have several advantages over vehicles with internal combustion engines (ICEs):

- **Energy efficient.** EVs convert about 59 to 62 percent of the electrical energy from the grid to power at the wheels—conventional gasoline vehicles only convert about 17 to 21 percent of the energy stored in gasoline to power at the wheels.
- **Environmentally friendly.** EVs emit no tailpipe pollutants. But the power plant producing the electricity may emit them. Electricity from nuclear-, hydro-, solar-, or wind-powered plants causes no air pollutants.

- **Performance benefits.** Electric motors provide quiet, smooth operation, stronger acceleration, and require less maintenance than ICEs.
- **Reduce energy dependence.** Electricity is a domestic energy source.[4]

Electric vehicles power up at a charging station. While these cars are very energy-efficient, they cannot go long distances between charges.

EVs do face some significant battery-related challenges:

- **Driving range:** Most EVs can only go about one hundred to two hundred miles before recharging. Gasoline vehicles can go over three hundred miles before refueling.
- **Recharge time:** Fully recharging the battery pack can take four to eight hours. Even a quick charge to 80 percent capacity can take as much as thirty minutes.

- **Battery cost:** The large battery packs are expensive and may need to be replaced one or more times.
- **Bulk and weight:** Battery packs are heavy and take up considerable space in the vehicle.

To date, researchers are working on improved battery technologies to increase driving range and decrease recharging time, weight, and cost. These factors will ultimately determine the future of EVs.[5]

DRIVING ON AIR

Meanwhile, other experts believe air-powered cars may become more attractive to consumers than electric cars. While both cars do a great job of cutting emissions, what makes a compressed air vehicle (CAV) more attractive than electric cars is the price. The CAV is expected to sell for about twenty thousand dollars, while electric cars can cost twice as much. CAVs work by compressing air instead of gasoline to move engine pistons.

The CAV also has a number of fuel options. For short commutes and in-town driving at up to thirty-five miles per hour, the car can go sixty miles on a tank of compressed air. For freeway driving, the CAV can travel at legal speeds for eight hundred miles using a small motor that compresses outside air to keep the tank filled. Meanwhile, the motor can burn just about anything—gasoline, ethanol, even cooking oil.[6]

Safety is a concern with the CAV. Experts wonder how these cars will do in crash tests. Many CAVs are small and made of light material that may not hold up as well in a crash as steel does.

DID YOU KNOW that idling at a drive-through window and in stop-and-go traffic costs motorists 753 million gallons (2,850 million liters) of gasoline a year, or $1,194 per driver in wasted fuel?[7]

RISING GAS PRICES

Aside from the fact that consumers want to go easy on the environment, the price of gasoline is also contributing to the popularity of hybrids, EVs, and CAVs. In fact, in the last ten years, the price of gasoline has quadrupled. As a result, Americans are driving fewer miles than ever, so

High prices at the gas pump are causing some people to consider hybrids and electric vehicles.

less gas is needed to power our cars. Larger vehicles like pickup trucks, minivans, and sport utility vehicles (SUVs) are less popular than ever before. In fact, sales for these vehicles have fallen below 50 percent for the first time since 2001.[8]

More than 75 percent of Americans are convinced that the rise in the price of gas they have experienced is permanent. And more than half of Americans believe that the price of gas will reach six dollars per gallon over the next five years. To deal with the rising prices, 71 percent say they are considering buying a more fuel-efficient vehicle.[9]

"With climate change concerns now, it's very likely that fuel efficiency will be at the forefront for the foreseeable future," says Samantha Gross, an energy research specialist. "It's unlikely we will go back to not caring about fuel efficiency the way we did in the late 1980s."[10]

DID YOU KNOW the Federal Highway Administration estimates that it costs people between twenty-two and twenty-nine cents per mile to drive a car depending on its size? But by carpooling every day, people can save up to three thousand dollars a year on gas, insurance, parking, and wear and tear on their car.[11]

HOMEGROWN FUEL

Many experts feel that biofuels, fuels made from plant materials, are part of the answer to addressing rising fuel costs, global warming, and our country's dependence on foreign oil. In fact, experts believe our dependence on oil from other countries is also impacting our nation's security and its economy. Many think that biofuels can help free Americans from this dependence. Biofuels also create rural jobs and improve opportunities for farmers. And if the technology is perfected it could also impact global warming.

Currently, ethanol, which is made from corn kernels, is the primary biofuel being used in this country. But because producing ethanol competes with corn for food products, can lead to deforestation, and requires lots of water, experts are looking for other types of biofuels. For instance, prairie grasses such as switchgrass, which occur naturally and are not food products, can produce a lot of cellulose. Cellulose can in turn be made into biofuel. However, the challenge is that cellulose is a lot more difficult to break down and turn into ethanol than corn. Other options include municipal trash, agricultural waste, algae, and

Ethanol is a biofuel made from corn kernels. While biofuels can help reduce or oil dependency, critics argue that using farmland for fuels causes deforestation and contributes to world hunger.

even carbon dioxide. But none of the technologies have been demonstrated to be feasible.

As a result, some say biofuels may be doing the opposite of what was hoped. For instance, using land to grow fuel causes the destruction of forests, wetlands, and grasslands. The trees and plants in these natural areas store enormous amounts of carbon. When they are destroyed, the amount of carbon released into the atmosphere increases. "It turns out that the carbon lost when wilderness is [cut down] overwhelms the gains from cleaner-burning fuels," writes Michael Grunwald, in "The Clean Energy Scam," an article in the April 7, 2008, issue of *TIME* magazine.[12]

Grunwald goes on to explain that the large demand for farm-grown fuels has raised world food prices and endangered the hungry. For instance, he says, "The grain it takes to fill an SUV with ethanol could feed a person for a year."[13] As a result, the United Nation's World Food Program says the rising cost of food is a global emergency and they need $500 million in additional funding and supplies. Lester Brown of the Earth Policy Institute says, "Biofuels pit the 800 million people with cars against the 800 million people with hunger problems."[14]

"The lesson behind the math is that on a warming planet, land is . . . incredibly precious . . . and every acre used to [make] fuel is an acre that can't be used to [make] the food needed to feed us or the carbon storage needed to save us," Grunwald writes.[15]

REDUCING EMISSION WITH FUEL EFFICIENCY

The government has also started to take fuel efficiency more seriously. The legislation passed in 2007 by George W. Bush required automakers

TAKE ACTION!
TRAVEL GREEN

You may be wondering: "What can I possibly do? I don't even own a car!" But you do not have to own a car or even be able to drive to conserve energy. You do not even have to convince your parents to buy a hybrid to have a positive impact. In fact, the small steps you take toward energy conservation can go a long way in reducing emissions. Here are some ideas:

- Skip the drive-through window at the fast-food restaurant and go inside.
- Turn off the car! When a car idles for more than ten seconds it actually uses more gas and creates more pollution than restarting the engine.[16]
- Carpool with neighbors or friends or ride the bus. For instance, the National Safety Council says that one full forty-foot bus takes fifty-eight cars off the road.[17]
- Encourage family and friends to drive slower. Not only are slower speeds safer, but the EPA estimates that every five miles per hour you drive over sixty miles per hour costs another twenty cents per gallon of gas.[18]
- Ask your parents to remove the car's roof rack. The Rocky Mountain Institute estimates that you can save fifteen to thirty gallons of gasoline a year by just leaving the rack off half the time.[19]
- Get your mom or dad a gift certificate for a tune-up on their next birthday. According to the EPA, a well-tuned engine can save thirteen cents a gallon. A clean air filter can save thirty-two cents a gallon, and properly inflated tires can save ten cents a gallon.[20]

to address fuel efficiency. Under the law, automakers must increase fuel efficiency by 40 percent. This increase will require cars, SUVs, and small trucks to get thirty-five miles (fifty-six kilometers) per gallon by 2020.

"We make a major step . . . toward reducing our dependence on oil, fighting global climate change, expanding the production of renewable fuels and giving future generations . . . a nation that is stronger, cleaner, and more secure," President Bush said.[21]

Meanwhile, the Obama Administration established tougher fuel economy standards for passenger vehicles in the United States. These standards require an average performance of 54.5 miles per gallon by 2025. The guidelines for heavy-duty trucks, buses and vans will reduce greenhouse gas emissions by about 270 million metric tons and save 530 million barrels of oil.[22]

CHAPTER 5

GREENER SCHOOLS

TEACHING YOUNG CHILDREN THE IMPORTANCE OF caring for the earth is as important as teaching them to tie their shoes or brush their teeth. Christy Radanof, creator of the Go for the Green Challenge program, believes that if children learn to care for the world around them it will become an automatic part of their life. She also wants children to feel empowered. Even though they are young, kids can still impact the world around them.

> As a parent, I saw Earth Day come and go several years in a row with very little if any mention in the classroom. And as a substitute teacher, I understand that there is so much information that teachers have to get through and only so much time in the day to do it. I wanted to develop a program that would be simple to incorporate into their day, wouldn't require more than a couple minutes a day, but that would encourage and empower the kids with the knowledge that they can create change.[1]

Students celebrate Earth Day by planting a tree.
Many believe that learning to take care of the earth
will help young people treat it more responsibly.

The Go for the Green Challenge contains a number of different elements. First, each classroom selected a green ambassador to be the liaison between the classroom and Radanof. Additionally, the green ambassadors kept their classmates on task and developed ideas on what they could do to impact the environment. They also made sure the classroom recycled paper and reduced its energy use by turning off lights and equipment.

Meanwhile, teachers were presented with a number of different tools. Radanof developed worksheets and arranged for the kids to become members of the EPA Kids Club. Each teacher received a list of books for their classrooms and websites the classes could visit. Radanof also arranged for the teachers to use the materials provided by *Meet The Greens*. "*Meet The Greens* is a cartoon . . . about different energy and environmental issues," Radanof says. "The teachers could show the cartoon and then there would be a quiz afterwards that the kids could take as a group and learn a little more."

The goal for each classroom was to meet all the challenges on their list and win a Green Tiger Paw for their classroom. "Everybody was kind of competing with each other to see who would get the Green Tiger Paw first," explains Radanof. "In the end, every single classroom ended up with the Green Tiger Paw. That was really exciting because I had set a goal that 60 percent of the school would get their Green Tiger Paw. But everyone ended up on board!"

As a reward, each student got a tree to plant at home. Initially, Radanof had planned to give each classroom a couple of trees and draw for the winners. But she was so pleased with the results that she wanted everyone to be rewarded. "I wanted each kid to see immediate benefits for doing something for the environment," she explains. "Many times when you take action to help the environment, you don't see results for a while. I wanted the kids to see some immediate benefit for their efforts."

GO GREEN PROGRAM INSPIRATION

Radanof says her inspiration for the challenge came from Dr. Wangari Maathai, an environmentalist and activist. In 2004 Maathai became the first African woman to receive the Nobel Peace Prize for "her contribution to sustainable development, democracy, and peace," says Radanof. She explained:

> When she was growing up, Dr. Maathai noticed that the water, crops, and animals were disappearing in her small South African country. And she had this brainstorm that there was a connection between that and all the trees her countrymen were cutting down. So what she decided to do was to teach women how to plant trees. She encouraged those women to take it to the different tribes and to plant trees. As a result, the landscape of her country was totally changed. They have water, crops, a forest and the animals are back. What amazed me was that she was one person who took it upon herself to encourage others.

Radanof believes that everyone can have the same impact if they share ideas. "Throughout the challenge, I make a strong point that kids need to communicate their ideas. Kids have fantastic ideas, but no one can act on them if they don't share them with others."

GREENER BUSING

Twenty-three million kids ride school buses each year. Yet the air inside the bus may actually be worse than the air outside. Yale researchers

Studies have shown that the air inside many school buses contains a high level of toxins. The buses also cause a lot of pollution. Laws have been passed that require lowering emissions in these buses.

found that the air inside diesel school buses had five to fifteen times more toxins than outside air.[2] Another study found that levels of diesel exhaust inside a school bus can be four times higher than those in cars driving just ahead of the bus.[3]

Exposure to diesel fumes is not uncommon. The vast majority of school buses still use diesel fuel even though less harmful fuels are available. In fact, many school districts still use old models, including buses built in the 1980s. Changing behaviors is one way to reduce the impact buses have on the environment. For instance, cutting down on the amount of time a school bus spends idling helps reduce harmful emissions and can save money.

Experts recommend that school officials adopt policies about idling. Some examples include:

- When loading and unloading children, the school bus should be turned off.
- Early-morning warm-up should be limited to idling no more than three to five minutes except in extreme weather.
- Buses should not be permitted to idle while waiting for students during field trips and extracurricular activities.
- The "cleanest" buses should be assigned the longest routes.

Recently, the EPA passed new emission standards for buses. Under the new standards, buses built after 2007 are required to release 90 percent less soot and 95 percent less emissions.

To do this, schools can either replace the buses with alternative fuel buses or retrofit existing buses. Retrofitting a bus involves putting a particle filter on the bus that helps reduce emissions. Switching fuels improves air quality as well. For instance, the Wissahickon School District switched to low-sulfur emission fuel.

"We've already started using a low-sulfur emission fuel," says Joe Malseed, the head mechanic for the district. "What will happen is as the vehicles start using it, it will clean their engines. We're hoping it will reduce emissions from 18 to 30 percent per bus."[4]

DID YOU KNOW that if you reduce the amount of time idling by ten minutes each day, you can keep 550 pounds (250 kilograms) of carbon dioxide out of the air every year?[5]

GREENER SCHOOLS

Operating a school costs a lot of money—many school districts pay more for energy than for supplies and books. In fact, K-12 schools in the United States spend more than $6 billion a year on energy. But according to the US Department of Energy, at least a quarter of that could be saved by conserving and managing energy better. This would cut the nation's school energy costs by $1.5 billion each year.[6]

One way schools can save money is by changing behavior. By simply turning off lights and computers, schools can save thousands of dollars. In fact, lighting is responsible for 50 percent of the electric bill in most schools.[7] Another way to lower lighting costs is to keep lights clean. Dirt and dust can reduce the amount of output from lights by as much as 15 percent a year.[8] Replacing the plastic covers, or diffusers, on lights also helps improve light output.

> **DID YOU KNOW** that a heavy coat of dust on a lightbulb can block up to half the light?[9]

Exit signs are another area where lighting costs can be reduced. For example, replacing exit signs that use incandescent lights with light-emitting diodes (LED) can save money. LEDs can last twenty-five years without needing to be replaced, compared to one year for incandescent lights. What's more, LED lights pay for themselves in less than a year in lower energy costs.

Even making changes to vending machines can save money. When a vending machine operates continuously, it can cost a school $200 to $350 a year. However, some companies make energy-control devices for vending machines that can save schools as much as 47 percent. Turning off the lights in the vending machine is another way to save money. For instance, Seattle School District saved $20,000 a year by turning off the lights in its 250 vending machines.[10]

Another way schools can save money is through daylighting, in which sunlight is captured on the rooftop and redirected to interior spaces, often using reflective tubes. According to the Sustainable Buildings Industry Council, the average middle school that uses daylighting will save tens of thousands of dollars annually. The research also suggests an improvement in student performance. In fact, one study found that students who attend daylit schools for two or more years scored 14 percent better on tests than students in schools that did not use daylighting.[11]

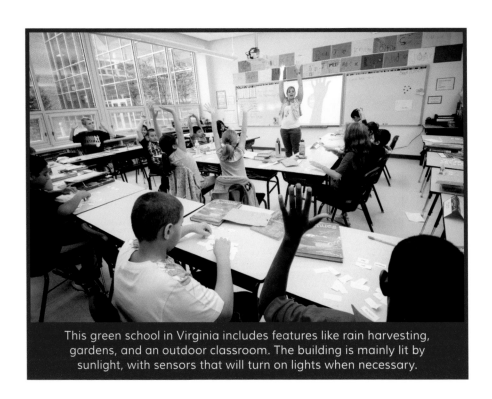

This green school in Virginia includes features like rain harvesting, gardens, and an outdoor classroom. The building is mainly lit by sunlight, with sensors that will turn on lights when necessary.

Finally, experts recommend that when school districts are constructing new buildings that they build green—especially since energy-efficient schools do not cost more to build. Schools that are designed to save energy and reduce their environmental impact can save the district 50 percent on energy bills compared to traditional schools.[12]

High-performance green schools typically use daylighting, have renewable energy systems, and include water conservation and recycling features. The Durant Road Middle School in Raleigh, North Carolina, is such a school. They use daylighting as well as a radiant barrier on the roof that reflects the sun's heat. As a result, the amount of air conditioning

LET THE SUN SHINE IN

Nineteen schools in South Carolina received a solar power system in 2006 for their school and an accompanying teaching program. This system was provided by Santee Cooper and the Electric Cooperatives of South Carolina, Inc., and is designed to teach students about renewable energy.

"Santee Cooper has been a leader in renewable energy," says Lonnie Carter, president and chief executive officer of the company. "This solar school program allows us to show not only children, but educators, the effectiveness of renewable energy options and the challenges associated with meeting current energy needs."[13]

The project also includes a renewable energy curriculum. The curriculum incorporates teaching, research, and hands-on opportunities. It is also supplemented by an Internet-based monitoring system that provides information about the system's performance.

required by the school is about 30 percent below that needed by a traditional school, so the school saves tens of thousands of dollars in energy costs each year.[14]

DID YOU KNOW that only 10 percent of the electricity used by an incandescent lightbulb is turned into light? The other 90 percent is wasted as heat.[15]

GREEN SAVINGS

One report makes the following suggestions for schools to cut energy costs:

Lighting strategies

- Schools can save anywhere from 8 to 20 percent on lighting by turning off lights in unoccupied rooms.
- Cleaning lamps and light fixtures regularly can save up to 15 percent on lighting.

Computers and Office Equipment

- Energy Star monitors have a low-power sleep mode that uses only between two and ten watts.
- Energy Star copiers can save schools 40 percent compared to standard models.

Maintenance

- Proper boiler maintenance can lead to energy savings of 10 to 20 percent.

TAKE ACTION!
MAKE YOUR SCHOOL GREEN

As a student, you have a vested interest in helping your school save money. If your school spends less money on energy, it will have more money for educational programs and activities. But you do not have to convince your school board to build a new school to have an impact. Little things add up, too. Below are some simple ways you can encourage your school's teachers and staff members to help cut energy costs.

- Ask your teacher if you can conduct a class experiment to see where there are drafts. Once you have determined the drafty areas, the class can make long thin cloth bags and fill them with beans to use as insulation along windows and doors.

- Form an energy patrol with your school's permission. Write down all the things in the school that use energy from the lights to the refrigerator in the teacher's lounge to the computers in the library. Submit ideas for how the school can lower energy costs by turning things off when they are not being used.

- Ask your teacher if you can print your reports on both sides of the paper. This not only saves paper, but cuts down on the energy used printing the report.

- Look for ways your school can reduce paper and submit your ideas to the principal. For instance, can the school newsletter be sent via e-mail? Or can your parents send electronic notes to the teacher instead of handwritten notes?

- Timers can be installed to shut off electric hot water tanks when the building is not occupied.

Kitchen/Vending

- Schools can reduce energy consumption by preheating ovens for no more than fifteen minutes before use.
- An energy control device for vending machines can save as much as 47 percent with payback of less than two years.[16]

CHAPTER 6

GREENER COMMUNITIES

ROCKETING THROUGH THE TOWN AT 205 MILES (330 kilometers) per hour, the May 2007 tornado that ripped through Greensburg, Kansas, was the one of the worst in US history. More than a mile and a half wide, it claimed the lives of eleven people. Sidewalks and underground sewers were all that remained.[1]

After the tornado, the townspeople had a decision to make. Either they could move on, or they could rebuild Greensburg and make it stronger—and greener. About half of the fifteen hundred residents decided to stay and build. Their commitment was to rebuild the town "as a showcase of environmentally friendly living." As a result, the town investigated ways to use renewable energy. Businesses and residents were encouraged to build energy-efficient homes.[2]

"If you are going to build a community from the ground up, it is our responsibility to think about the future," says City Administrator Steve Hewitt.[3] Kim Alderfer, assistant city manager, added, "I would never say

The 2007 tornado that struck Greensburg, Kansas,
almost destroyed the entire town.

the tornado happening was a good thing. I would never wish that on anybody. But given the opportunity, we have to do it right—to make it better."[4]

It took some work to get everyone on board, says Daniel Wallach, who formed the nonprofit group Greensburg GreenTown. He says they showed residents that going green was about more than saving polar bears. It also involves cutting waste, saving on energy costs, and building a stronger town. Those arguments made sense. "Our church sometimes costs up to $1,000 a month to heat," says Marvin George, pastor of a Baptist church in the town. He says he hopes to rebuild the church to meet the highest energy efficiency standards.[5]

"Self-sufficiency and independence are strong values out here. Farmers and ranchers all make their living from the land, so they have an awareness and sensitivity to it that is unique," says Wallach.[6]

And although the rebuilding process is slow, it is moving forward. The 4,700-square-foot (437-square-meter) city hall building has opened. Located in the heart of the town, it has become a symbol of the community's commitment to become a model for sustainable communities everywhere. The building gathers solar energy, collects rainwater for reuse on-site and makes maximum use of daylight. The town hopes this building will receive a LEED Platinum Certification.[7]

LEED, which stands for Leadership in Energy and Environmental Design, is a rating system. It was developed by the US Green Building Council and sets standards for sustainable construction. LEED Platinum buildings cost about 5 percent more to construct, says Jack Rozdilsky, a University of North Texas professor who has studied Greensburg's rebuilding effort. But, he says the buildings typically have 30 to 50 percent lower energy bills.[8]

Greensburg has already captured the nation's attention and their hearts. President George W. Bush spoke at the graduation commencement for the town's eighteen high school seniors—something he had never done before. And Leonardo DiCaprio produced a thirteen-part series about the town. It is called *Eco-Town* and aired on the Discovery Channel. Furthermore, the National Building Museum featured a one-year exhibit on the town's rebuilding efforts.

"They are really making a wonderful opportunity out of an absolute tragedy," says Susan Piedmont, museum curator and architect. She adds that having small towns like Greensburg embrace environmentally friendly architecture will help people see how easy environmental building can be.[9]

What impresses people most is the town's vision and optimism despite suffering a tragic loss. "Ninety percent of the town was just gone overnight, and yet the social fabric was intact even without the

Bob Dixson, Mayor of Greensburg, stands in the middle of the largely rebuilt town in 2014. Greensburg's new motto is "Stronger, Better, Greener."

buildings," says Stephen Hardy, a city planner with the architectural firm BNIM.[10] It is this social fabric that allows a town like Greensburg to rebound like it has.

"You don't experience a storm like this and come out of it with an attitude of complacency," says Wallach.[11] "People from around the country and around the world will come [to Greensburg] to see what the future looks like."[12]

MOVING TOWARD GREENER COMMUNITIES

A healthy community is the cornerstone of a healthy society. It is the place where people connect with one another—where they live, work, play, and learn. As a result, experts say that sustainable communities are becoming more attractive because people realize that if they work together, they can produce a higher quality of life.

According to the Natural Resources Defense Council, people are recognizing that development is "gobbling up the American countryside at an alarming rate." In fact, each hour, about 365 acres of open land is turned into "strip malls, anonymous suburbs, and traffic-clogged roads."[13] As a result, some communities are choosing to develop differently. They are looking to become sustainable.

In communities that sustain themselves, businesses, households, and government make efficient use of land, energy, and other resources, allowing the area to improve life with minimal waste and environmental damage. These communities are healthy and secure, and provide people with clean air to breathe and safe water to drink, according to the Civic Renewal Movement of the Civic Practices Network (CPN): "In sustainable communities, people are engaged in building a community together. They are well-informed and actively involved in making community decisions. They make decisions for the long term that benefit future generations as well as themselves."[14]

BENEFITS OF GREENER COMMUNITIES

How and where we build has a huge environmental impact. According to Greener Communities, buildings account for 38 percent of annual carbon dioxide emissions, 30 percent of both raw materials waste and landfill waste, and 12 percent of potable water consumption. But if communities make a commitment to become sustainable, they can reverse these trends. This requires environmentally responsible planning and building as well as the creation of energy-efficient and water-efficient buildings. One way this is accomplished is by using renewable resources such as solar and geothermal energy. This in turn reduces carbon dioxide.

Sustainable communities also strive to conserve natural resources by choosing materials that are renewable, recycled, and durable when constructing homes and other buildings. They reduce waste through the reuse and recycling of materials.[15]

> **DID YOU KNOW** that nearly half of the greenhouse gas emissions in the United States come from buildings?[16]

EXAMPLES OF GREENER COMMUNITIES

If you look across the nation, you will see varying degrees of sustainability. Some communities have been sustainable for years while others are just

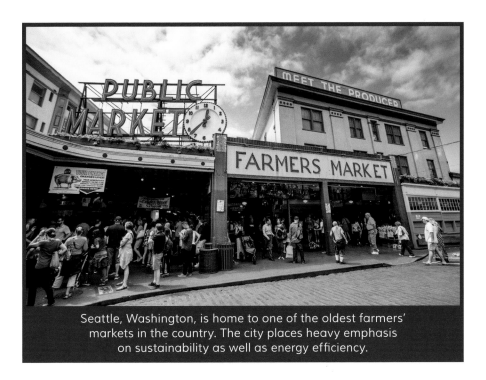

Seattle, Washington, is home to one of the oldest farmers' markets in the country. The city places heavy emphasis on sustainability as well as energy efficiency.

getting started. Listed below are three communities—each addressing sustainability but each at different stages.

Seattle, Washington

Seattle was one of the first cities in the United States to incorporate the ideas of sustainability into community planning. According to the volunteer civic organization Sustainable Seattle, a sustainable city is one that "thrives without compromising the ability of future generations to meet their needs."[17]

Experts explain that an important part of Seattle's sustainable city definition is the concept of the city as a system within a system. In other words, they want neighborhoods to do well within the city. As a result, decision making is done by considering the effects on the entire system and on future generations.

Since 1990, many new city policies, plans, and programs have included sustainability. For instance, Seattle has been working with industries in the area. As a result, the city and Boeing, a company that makes airplanes, agreed to use waste heat from a new sewer trunk line to provide heat for the company. This saves on the cost of both heating equipment and fuel.

Experts say that many of Seattle's most successful sustainability projects have been city- and county-sponsored programs. These programs train volunteers so they can teach others about more sustainable practices. Some of the programs have included Friends of Recycling, Master Composters, and Master Gardeners. What's more, many small businesses are implementing more sustainable practices, including everything from eco-retailers to bicycling carpet cleaners.

Burlington, Vermont

In 2007 Burlington was ranked as one of the top metropolitan areas by *Country Home* magazine and received the Best Green Places award. The magazine rated cities based on air quality, mass transit use, power use, and the number of organic producers and farmers' markets. Second place went to Ithaca, New York, and Corvallis, Oregon, took third place. "We thought to ourselves, 'If we could live anywhere in the United States, where would be the best green place to live?'" says Grant Fairchild, managing editor.[18] Burlington received especially high marks for the way its people, businesses, and government value green living. Among Burlington's green features are the following:

- A compost facility collects food scraps from restaurants, supermarkets, and food manufacturers and sells the compost to farmers, gardeners, and landscapers.

- The area has sixteen farmers' markets, five producers of organic food, and three food co-ops.
- Carpools are used by 12.3 percent of Burlington-area commuters, about 5.6 percent of the workforce walks to work, and 4.6 percent work at home.[19]

"It's certainly an honor to be called the greenest city in America," says Betsy Rosenbluth, project director for Burlington Legacy, the sustainable city initiative. "Burlington . . . really understands the connection between our environment and our economy and our social health."[20]

Chicago, Illinois

In September 2008, Mayor Richard M. Daley announced a plan for Chicago to become one of the greenest cities in the nation. The plan calls for reducing greenhouse gas emissions to three-fourths of 1990 levels by 2020. To get there, the city will address energy efficiency, using clean and renewable energy sources, improving transportation, and reducing pollution.

"We can't solve the world's climate change problem in Chicago, but we can do our part," says Daley. "We have a shared responsibility to protect our planet."[21] Daley is one of about eight hundred mayors who have agreed to adopt that goal. But Chicago was the first to identify specific pollution sources and outline how it would achieve the reductions. For instance, the city has an agreement with two coal-fired power plants to reduce emissions or shut down by 2015 and 2017.

The plan also calls for increasing recycling and carpooling, promoting alternative fuels, and expanding the number of green rooftops. Also called living rooftops, green rooftops contain living plants. The rooftop may contain grass, shrubs, flowers, and sometimes even trees if it can support the weight.

All in all, there is growing interest in sustainable communities. But experts say until we can get legislators, like those in Chicago, Seattle, and Burlington, to enact policies that encourage their development, it is going to be a challenge to produce green communities.

A groundskeeper tends to a rooftop garden on top of City Hall in Chicago.

TAKE ACTION!
MAKING YOUR COMMUNITY GREENER

As a young person, you may be wondering what you can do to help your community become more sustainable. Here are a few ideas to help you get started. Remember, communities become sustainable when each community member does his or her part.

- **Plant a tree.** According to AmericanForests.org, planting trees around your home can conserve energy and lower costs. In fact, planting large deciduous trees on the east, west, and northwest sides of your home creates shade and reduces summer air conditioning costs by up to 35 percent.[22]

- **Bring your own bags to the grocery.** Plastic shopping bags often end up littering community streets. They also get tangled in treetops, choke animals, and clog sewer systems. And if they ever do make it to a landfill, they take years to decompose.

- **Ask your parents if you can recycle rainwater.** If you use a rain barrel to hold the rainwater falling on your property, you can help reduce flooding and pollution in the storm water system.

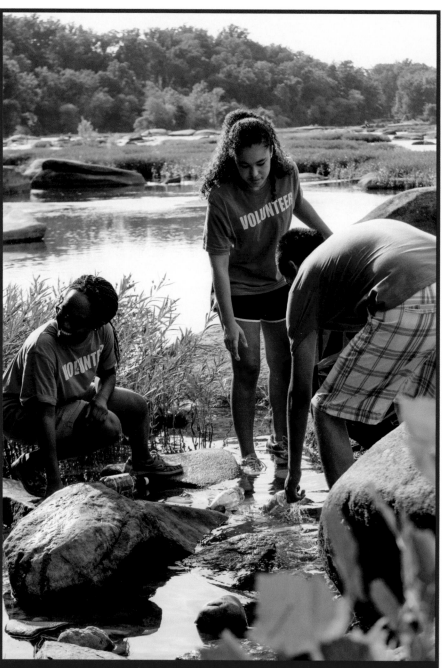

Young people must get actively involved to make a difference with climate change. Recycling and picking up trash are just a few small ways you can make a contribution.

CHAPTER 7

GREEN OR GRIM FUTURE? IT'S UP TO YOU

CLIMATE CHANGE IS NOT A NEW IDEA. IN FACT, SCIENTISTS have been warning Americans for years what could happen if we do not change the way we use energy. Still, studies indicate that many Americans think climate change is a topic that scientists do not agree about. In reality, research shows that about 97 percent of climate scientists conclude that humans are changing the climate.[1]

It has taken years for people to buy into the fact that the climate is changing and we need to do something about it today. A large part of the delay is due to the way in which climate change has been presented. "Green-minded activists failed to move the . . . public not because they were wrong, but because the solutions they offered were unappealing," says Alex Nikolai Steffen, author of *Worldchanging: A User's Guide for the*

21st Century. "They rejected technology, business and prosperity in favor of . . . a simpler way of life."[2]

Today, a new green movement is taking shape. Steffen says it is a movement that embraces environmental concerns but offers different answers to the problems. For instance, he says that business, technology, scientific exploration, and sustainable policies "can propel the world into a bright green future." He continues:

> Americans trash the planet not because we are evil but because the . . . systems we've devised leave no other choice . . . Our ranch houses and high-rises, factories and farms, freeways and power plants were [developed] before we had a clue how the planet works . . . [But] tomorrow we might see vehicles that consume no fossil fuels and emit no greenhouse gases. Combine cars like that with smarter urban growth and we're well on our way to sustainable transportation.[3]

THE CLOCK IS TICKING

Naomi Klein, author of *This Changes Everything*, agrees that changing the way we do things has to start now. She points out that climate change is a wake-up call for our country. It is a powerful message, she says, delivered in wildfires, floods, storms, and droughts. Addressing it is no longer just about changing lightbulbs and recycling. It is about changing the world.

> We know that if we continue on our current path of allow-ing emissions to rise year after year, climate change will

change everything about our world. Major cities will very likely drown, ancient cultures will be swallowed by the seas, and there is a very high chance [that you will spend a great deal of your life] fleeing and recovering from vicious storms and extreme droughts. And we don't have to do anything to bring about this future. All we have to do is nothing.[4]

Klein adds that if we continue denying how frightening climate change is, then little by little, we will come to the place that we most fear. We will experience "the thing from which we have been averting our eyes. No additional effort required," she says.[5]

According to Klein, there are ways of preventing this grim future. But, she says, the catch involves changing everything. "For us high consumers it involves changing how we live, how our economies function, even the stories we tell about our place on earth," she says. "The good news

Marchers in New York City protest for more action against climate change in 2014.

is that many of these changes are distinctly un-catastrophic. Many are downright exciting."[6]

CHANGE BEGINS WITH YOU

Some experts believe that this green movement will be pushed forward by young people like you. It is no secret that kids can be passionate about issues. From the civil rights movement in the 1960s to the no nukes movement in the 1970s and outrage over child labor in the 1980s, students have had the ability to change history.

The same is true with the global climate movement. It is time for serious change in the United States.

Moving the government to change will require coordinated action and a smart use of the Internet, says Bill McKibben, an author and environmentalist.[7] For instance, he and a number of students developed a virtual march on Washington in April 2007. They called it *Step It Up National Day of Climate Action*, and they organized more than fourteen hundred communities to get their message out. In each location, participants held up banners that said *Step It Up, Congress: Cut Carbon 80 percent by 2050*. Photos from these locations streamed to the web from all across the country. Some material was even streamed from underwater in Key West, from the dwindling glaciers in Wyoming, and from the levees of New Orleans.[8]

McKibben believes that because your generation will suffer the consequences of climate change, your efforts toward a greener America will make a difference. "There are a lot of people who are educated about global warming and want to figure out what to do," he says. "The students, ultimately, are the mainstream-in-training."[9]

CHANGING YOUR PERSPECTIVE

The first step in impacting change is changing your own perspective and behaviors. For instance, Klein identifies four areas where people's perspectives should change, including slowing down, consuming less, believing in climate change, and sharing the story.

1. **Slow down.** Many people do not realize that climate change is occurring because they race through life without paying attention to the little changes, says Klein. But climate change is happening all around us if we just slow down and pay attention. She says climate change is measured in "receding ice sheets, swelling waters and incremental temperature rises."

2. **Consume less.** According to Klein, climate change is not a problem that can be solved by simply changing what we buy, such as a hybrid vehicle instead of an SUV. It also means as a whole American consumers are going to have to consume less of everything they purchase. From houses and transportation to clothing, food, and entertainment, Klein says the consumption in America needs to slow down.

3. **Start believing.** Pollutants are invisible. As a result, most people have stopped believing in what they cannot see, says Klein. They buy into the belief that what we cannot see will not hurt us or that it may not exist at all. But climate change is real and it can hurt us. It is time to stop burying our head in the sand and hoping someone else will do something about it.

4. **Share the story.** Klein emphasizes that people must talk more about climate change and how it is impacting the local communities where we live. The goal is that our daily existence would be more connected to the physical places where we live and what is going on around us.[10]

TAKE ACTION!
GET INVOLVED

If you want to get more involved in reducing climate change and helping make the world around you a greener place, hook up with one of the many nonprofits dedicated to helping young people advocate for the environment. Here are just a few of your options:

- **Earthforce, Inc.,** helps kids ages ten to fourteen develop citizenship skills while addressing both local and national environmental problems.

- **SustainUS** is a group that focuses on sustainable development. Through its Agents of Change program it sends young delegates to United Nations conferences on climate change, sustainable development and other similar issues. Meanwhile, its Lead Now Fellowship trains young people to become leaders in sustainable development.

- **Youth for Environmental Sanity (YES!)** runs summer camps devoted to teaching kids how to take action on behalf of the environment. They also hold JAMS, which bring together local change-makers to brainstorm solutions for environmental issues.

GETTING OUT OF THE HOLE

Ask any American and you will probably find that he supports increased energy conservation, less drilling, and more renewable energy sources. In fact, creating alternative energy sources is more important to most Americans than expanding exploration of oil, coal and natural gas by a ratio of two to one.

At the same time, more Americans oppose the increased use of fracking to extract oil and natural gas from underground rock formations than favor it. And 8 percent want the government to require better fuel efficiency for cars, trucks and SUVs.

Get involved any way you can! These Colorado teens are distributing environmentally friendly lightbulbs in neighborhoods. Young people can be at the forefront in promoting clean, green energy.

While the majority of people favor developing alternative sources of energy, opinions vary widely depending on the age group. Adults under

TAKE ACTION!
DIGITAL ACTIVISM

We have entered an age of digital activism where movements like addressing climate change are created through tweets, blogs, status updates, YouTube videos, and more. In fact, research shows that two out of five young people are engaging with social issues online. They are using Facebook and Twitter to provide first-hand accounts and live updates on things that are happening in their area related to an issue close to their heart.[11]

According to experts, this trend grew from a genuine faith in the power of the Internet. In fact, one study indicates that two out of three Millennials believe "that a person on a computer, being aware and spreading the word" is capable of sparking more change than a person on the street at a rally or a protest.[12]

Helping encourage teen activism are groups like DoSomething.org, a nonprofit organization that helps empower young people to develop campaigns that tackle just about any issue of importance to them. "A lot of teens do not know where to start," says Colleen Wormsley, a marketing associate with the organization. "We show them different ways to take action in hopes that it will be a lifelong habit."[13]

Consider what you want to do to address climate change using social media and the Internet. For instance, you could develop a Twitter account designed to increase awareness about climate change. Or you could blog about current issues related to climate change. You could even develop videos for YouTube with tips for others on how to change their behaviors in simple ways that will impact climate change. The options are endless!

thirty express strong support for prioritizing alternative energy development (74 percent to 20 percent). By contrast, those sixty-five and older are divided on the subject. Forty-eight percent favor developing energy sources such as wind, solar and hydrogen while 41 percent feel expanding production of oil, coal and natural gas should be given more priority.[14]

Finally, most Americans say they are open to changing to protect the environment. For instance, 61 percent said they would rather pay more for cleaner fuels than pay less for fuels that pollute. And more than 60 percent said they would accept wind terminals and solar plants in their hometowns.[15]

CHANGING THE WORLD'S PERSPECTIVE

Changing behaviors is challenging; it is always easier to continue what you are doing than to change your ways. Yet it is clear that many Americans care about the environment and conserving energy. They seem ready to embrace green power as a means of getting there. "[But] meeting science-based targets will mean forcing some of the profitable companies on the planet to forfeit trillions of dollars of future earnings by leaving the vast majority of proven fossil fuel reserves in the ground," says Klein.[16]

But the longer we wait to respond, the more risks that climate change will increase. The emissions of greenhouse gases today commit the planet to unavoidable climate change in the future. Fortunately, America's young people like you are some of the most innovative and resourceful in the world. When you recognize the dire need for change, you can channel your passion and your energy to solve this problem.

According to Klein, the country's only hope is mass social movement toward change. This movement begins with you. Her advice is to help block the roads that are causing the climate to change and at the same time help clear the path for safer alternatives. "If that happens, well, [you] change everything," she says.[17]

APPENDIX

EXCERPT FROM *WHAT WE KNOW: THE REALITY, RISKS, *and Response to Climate Change*, by Advancing Science, Serving Society (AAAS), 2014

CLIMATE REALITY

A. Climate scientists agree: Humans are driving climate change.

In 2013, only 42% of American adults understood that "most scientists think global warming is happening" and 33% said, ". . . there is a lot of disagreement among scientists about whether or not global warming is happening." Twenty percent said they "don't know enough to say."

Even Americans who have come to recognize that climate change is occurring know there are limits to their ability to make this judgment from their own experiences. It might appear as if it's raining more or less often, that it's hotter than usual, or that there are more storms than in the past. But is this true climate change or just natural variation? Does a particularly cold or snowy winter, such as the one the eastern United States experienced in 2013 and 2014, or variations in the rate of global surface temperature change call global warming into question? If the climate is changing, are human activities responsible, or is it being caused by natural factors?

Americans look to experts for guidance. If people believe the experts are in doubt about whether global warming is happening, it is no surprise that they will have less confidence in their own beliefs. Perceived expert disagreement has other consequences for the American people. Research shows that Americans who think the scientific experts disagree about human-caused climate change are less likely to believe that it might have serious consequences. Failure to appreciate the scientific consensus reduces support for a broad societal response to the challenges and risks that climate change presents.

So let us be clear: Based on well-established evidence, about 97% of climate scientists conclude that humans are changing the climate.

This widespread agreement is documented not by a single study but by a converging stream of evidence over the past two decades from polls of scientists, content analyses of peer-reviewed literature and from public statements issued by virtually every expert scientific membership organization on this topic. The evidence is overwhelming: Levels of greenhouse gases in the atmosphere are rising. Temperatures are going up. Springs are arriving earlier. Ice sheets are melting. Sea level is rising. The patterns of rainfall and drought are changing. Heat waves are getting worse, as is extreme precipitation. The oceans are acidifying.

The science linking human activities to climate change is analogous to the science linking smoking to lung and cardiovascular diseases. Physicians, cardiovascular scientists, public health experts, and others all agree smoking causes cancer. And this consensus among the health community has convinced most Americans that the health risks from smoking are real. A similar consensus now exists among climate scientists, a consensus that maintains that climate change is happening and that human activity is the cause. The National Academy of Sciences, for example, says that "the Earth system is warming and that much of this warming is very likely due to human activities."

B. Climate change is happening now. And it's going to get worse. No matter where they live, Americans are experiencing the effects of climate change. Of course, extreme weather events of varied intensity have always occurred. Family photo albums, community lore, and history books recount the big storms, droughts, and floods that communities have borne. Against this backdrop of natural variation, however, something different is happening. Greenhouse gases from manmade sources such as smokestacks and tailpipes have altered our climate system. Greenhouse gases have supercharged the climate, just as steroids supercharged hitting in Major League Baseball. Over the course of a baseball season in the steroid era, we witnessed more—and longer—home runs, even though we cannot attribute any specific homer to steroids. Similarly, even though we cannot attribute any particular weather event to climate change, some types of extreme events such as heat waves are now more frequent.

Extreme weather is not just an abstract concept. It is a reality that affects people across the country. In 2013, two out of three Americans said weather in the United States has been worse over the past several years, up twelve percentage points since spring 2012. Many (51%) say weather in their local area has been worse over the past several years. Not surprisingly, then, the gap between what we know as scientists (that global warming impacts are here and now) and what Americans perceive is narrowing: About six in ten Americans already say, "Global warming is affecting weather in the U.S."

To read the entire report, go to:

http://whatweknow.aaas.org/wp-content/uploads/2014/07/whatwe know_website.pdf

Excerpt from "Climate Change and President's Obama's Action Plan," released by the White House, 2014.

THE PRESIDENT'S PLAN TO CUT CARBON POLLUTION IN AMERICA

Reducing Carbon Pollution from Power Plants

Power plants are the largest major source of emissions in the U.S., together accounting for roughly one-third of all domestic greenhouse gas pollution.

PROGRESS: In September 2013, the Environmental Protection Agency (EPA) announced proposed carbon pollution standards for new power plants.

PROGRESS: In June 2014, EPA proposed the Clean Power Plan—the first-ever carbon pollution standards for existing power plants that will protect the health of our children and put our nation on the path toward a 30 percent reduction in carbon pollution from the power sector by 2030.

Accelerating Clean Energy Leadership

During the President's first term, the United States more than doubled generation of electricity from wind and solar energy.

PROGRESS: Since President Obama took office, the U.S. has increased solar generation by more than ten-fold and tripled electricity production from wind power.

PROGRESS: Since the President took office, the Department of the Interior has permitted over 50 wind, solar, and geothermal utility-scale projects on public or tribal lands. The projects could support over 20,000 jobs and generate enough electricity to power 4.8 million homes.

PROGRESS: DOE's Solar Instructor Training Network will support community college training programs to help 50,000 workers enter the solar industry by 2020. DOE's SunShot Solar Instructor Training Network is partnering with military bases to create a veterans solar job training pilot.

PROGRESS: Building on our progress in wind and solar, the Administration announced over 350 private and public-sector commitments to deploy over 885 MW of solar—enough to power over 130,000 homes—and cut energy waste in more than 1.4 billion square feet of U.S. buildings.

Building a 21st Century Clean Energy Infrastructure

Heavy-duty vehicles (commercial trucks, vans, and buses) are currently the second largest source of greenhouse gas pollution within the transportation sector.

PROGRESS: In January 2014, President Obama signed a Presidential Memorandum establishing the federal government's first Quadrennial Energy Review (QER) process, with an initial focus on our nation's energy infrastructure.

PROGRESS: In February 2014, President Obama directed EPA and DOT to develop and issue the next phase of heavy-duty vehicle fuel efficiency and greenhouse gas standards. The standards are proposed in March 2015 and finalized in March 2016.

PROGRESS: In 2011, the Administration finalized fuel economy standards for Model Year 2014-2018 for heavy-duty trucks, buses, and vans. This will reduce greenhouse gas emissions by about 270 million metric tons and save 530 million barrels of oil.

PROGRESS: The Administration has already established the toughest fuel economy standards for passenger vehicles in U.S. history. These standards require an average performance equivalent of 54.5 miles per gallon by 2025.

To read the entire report, go to:
https://www.whitehouse.gov/climate-change

CHAPTER NOTES

Chapter 1. Wasting Away

1. Christy Radanof, interview, September 2008. Unless otherwise indicated, all quotes from Radanof come from this interview.

2. "Use It and Lose It: The Outsize Effect of U.S. Consumption on the Environment," *Scientific American*, September 14, 2012, http://www.scientific american.com/article/american-consumption-habits/.

3. "Energy and You," United States Environmental Protection Agency, accessed June 2015, http://www.epa.gov/cleanenergy/energy-and-you/index.html.

4. Russell McLendon, "Where Does Coal Come From," *Mother Nature Network*, August 4, 2009, http://www.mnn.com/earth-matters/translating-uncle-sam/ stories/where-does-coal-come-from.

5. "How much oil consumed by the United States comes from foreign sources?" U.S. Energy Information Administration, accessed June 2015, http://www.eia .gov/tools/faqs/faq.cfm?id=32&t=6.

6. "Climate Change—Basic Information," US Environmental Protection Agency, February 16, 2010, www.epa.gov/climatechange/basicinfo.html.

7. "NASA Finds 2012 Sustained Long-Term Climate Warming Trend," NASA, January 15, 2013, http://www.nasa.gov/topics/earth/features/2012-temps.html.

8. Ibid.

9. "Climate Change—Basic Information," US Environmental Protection Agency.

10. Ibid.

11. Colleen Diskin, "Global Warming Lengthening Allergy Season," *NorthJersey .com*, April 18, 2008, www.northjersey.com/environment/17894024.html.

12. Bryan Walsh, "Allergies Getting Worse? Blame Global Warming," *TIME*, September 15, 2008, www.time.com/time/health/article/0,8599,1841125,00.html.

13. "Asthma," World Health Organization, accessed June 2015, http://www.who .int/mediacentre/factsheets/fs307/en/.

14. Bryan Walsh, "Allergies Getting Worse? Blame Global Warming."

15. Ibid.

16. Greenland Ice: The Warmer It Gets the Faster It Melts, *Science Daily*, accessed January 20, 2015, http://www.sciencedaily.com/releases/2015/01/150120151221 .htm.

17. Ibid.

18. "Global warming already killing," *Climate Ark*, November 1, 2006, http.www .climateark.org/shared/reader/welcome.aspx?linkid=64050.

19. Ibid.

Chapter 2. Things Are Getting Heated

1. About the Film, *An Inconvenient Truth*, accessed June 2015, http://www.takepart .com/an-inconvenient-truth/film.

2. "The Gore Factor: Reviewing the impact of *An Inconvenient Truth*," accesed June 2015, http://www.ecosmagazine.com/?act=view_file&file_id=EC134p16.pdf.

3. William J. Broad, "From a Rapt Audience, a Call to Cool the Hype," *The New York Times*, March 13, 2007, http://www.nytimes.com/2007/03/13/science/13gore .html?ex=1331438400&en=2df9d6e7a5aa6ed6&ei=5090&partner=rssuserland &emc=rss.

4. Ibid.

5. Ibid.

6. Ibid.

7. Ibid.

8. Ibid.

9. "Global Warming 101: The Science," Cooler Heads Coalition, February 4, 2009, http://www.globalwarming.org/2009/02/03/global-warming-101-science/.

10. Ibid.

11. Interview with Richard C. J. Sommerville, "What's Up with the Weather—The Debate," *PBS*, 2000, www.pbs.org/wgbh/warming/debate/.

12. "Green Power Defined," EPA Green Power Partnership, US Environmental Protection Agency, March 24, 2009, www.epa.gov/greenpower/gpmarket/index.htm.

13. "Kyoto and Beyond," *CBC News*, February 14, 2007, www.cbc.ca/news/background/kyoto/.

14. "Energy Efficiency and Renewable Energy," Solar Energy Technologies Program, U.S. Department of Energy, March 19, 2009.

15. "Going Green 101: Resources for Your Family," *The Oprah Winfrey Show*, April 20, 2007, www.oprah.com/article/oprahshow/tows_past_20070420_b.

16. "A Few Facts About Energy," National Association of Conservation Districts, accessed April 5, 2010, http://www.nacdnet.org/education/resources/energy/.

17. "Growing Energy on the Farm: Biomass and Agriculture," Union of Concerned Scientists, accessed April 5, 2010, http://www.ucsusa.org/clean_energy/technology_and_impacts/ impacts/growing-energy-on-the-farm.html.

18. "Hydroelectricty," US Environmental Protection Agency, accessed June 2015, http://www.epa.gov/cleanenergy/energy-and-you/affect/hydro.html.

19. "Grand Coulee Dam Statistics and Facts," US Department of Interior Bureau of Reclamation, accessed June 2015, http://www.usbr.gov/pn/grandcoulee/pubs/factsheet.pdf.

20. "The Geysers," Calpine Corporation, accessed June 2015, http://www.geysers.com/geothermal.aspx.

21. "Chicago Climate Exchange Closes Nation's First Cap-And-Trade System but Keeps Eye to the Future," *The New York Times*, January 3, 2011, http://www.nytimes.com/cwire/2011/01/03/03climatewire-chicago-climate-exchange-closes-but-keeps-ey-78598.html?pagewanted=all.

22. Ibid

23. Ibid.

24. "Municipal Solid Waste, United States Environmental Protection Agency, accessed June 2015, http://www.epa.gov/epawaste/nonhaz/municipal/index.htm.

25. Len Vermillion, "Sweeping Away Energy Waste," *Manufacturing.net*, May 22, 2007, www.manufacturing.net/sweeping-away-energy-waste.aspx?menuid=242.

26. Ibid.

27. "DOE Seeks Applications to Invest up to $40 Million in Housing Research," US Department of Energy, press release, June 13, 2007, www.energy.gov/news/5128.htm.

Chapter 3. Home Is Where the Green Is

1. Craig Pickerill, interview, September 2008. Unless otherwise indicated, all quotes from Pickerill come from this interview.

2. Len Vermillion, "Sweeping Away Energy Waste," *Manufacturing.net*, May 22, 2007, www.manufacturing.net/sweeping-away-energy-waste.aspx?menuid =242.

3. "Clothes Washers for Consumers," Energy Star, US Department of Energy, accessed June 2015, https://www.energystar.gov/products/certified-products/detail/clothes-washers.

4. David J. Lipke, "Green Homes—Eco-friendly Home Building Trends," Media Central, Inc., January 2001, http://findarticles.com/p/articles/mi_m4021/is_ISSN_0163-4089/ai_75171065.

5. "Carbon Offsets," President Homes, accessed November 2008, www.president homes.com/Services/GreenBuilding/Default.aspx.

6. "Green Building Is Now a Trend, Maybe One Near a Tipping Point," *Mortgage News Daily*, July 10, 2006, www.mortgagenewsdaily.com/7102006_Green_Building_Products.asp.

7. "Zero Energy Home Design," Energy Efficiency and Renewable Energy: US Department of Energy, April 22, 2009, http://apps1.eere.energy.gov/consumer/your_home/designing_remodeling/index.cfm/mytopic=10360.

8. "Buying Green Power," Green Power Network, Energy Efficiency and Renewable Energy, US Department of Energy, April 16, 2007.

9. "Buying Green Power."

10. Associated Press, "New Exhibit has Visitors Thinking Green," *CBS News*, August 1, 2008, www.cbsnews.com/stories/2008/08/01/tech/livinggreen/main4315954.shtml.

11. Ibid.

12. Ibid.

13. "Appliances by Day and Energy Vampires by Night: Save Energy by Cutting Your Phantom Loads," *Living Green Magazine*, August 1, 2013, http://living greenmag.com/2013/08/01/energy-ecology/appliances-by-day-and-energy-vampires-by-night-save-energy-by-cutting-your-phantom-loads/.

14. "Energy Facts," The Energy Coalition, accessed April 5, 2010, http://www.energycoalition.org/contents/energy-information-tips/energy-glossary.aspx.

15. Clayton Sandell, "Reducing Your Carbon Footprint," *ABC News*, June 7, 2006, http://abcnews.go.com/Technology/story?id=2049304&page=1.

16. Christy Radanof, interview, September 2008.

17. Jesse Ellison, "Save the Planet, Lose the Guilt," *Newsweek*, July 7–14, 2008, www.newsweek.com/143701.

18. Ibid.

19. Associated Press, "Bush Signs Bill Boosting Car Fuel Efficiency," *MSNBC*, December 19, 2007, www.msnbc.msn.com/id/22326795.

20. Ibid.

21. "Climate Change and President Obama's Action Plan," The White House, accessed June 2015, https://www.whitehouse.gov/climate-change.

22. Ibid.

23. Ibid.

24. "Living Green," Minnesota Pollution Control Agency, April 2015, http://www.pca.state.mn.us/index.php/living-green/citizens.html.

25. Ellison.

26. Ibid.

27. "Tips and Facts," Community Green: Environmental Leadership for Homeowners Associations, accessed April 5, 2010, http://www.caigreen.org/tips/.

28. Ellison.

29. "Did You Know?" Live Green, accessed April 5, 2010, http://newportlivegreen.com/LG-DidYou-Know.html.

30. "Sins of Greenwashing," United Laboratories, accessed June 2015, http://sinsofgreenwashing.com/about-us/index.html.

31. Ibid

32. Ibid.

33. Ibid

34. "Fifty Ways to go Green," *WNBC*, 2007, www.wnbc.com/print/12907475/detail.html.

35. "Did You Know?"

Chapter 4. Driving Green

1. Jennifer Kirk, interview, August 2008. Unless otherwise indicated, all quotes from Kirk come from this interview.

2. Cobb, Jeff. "Americans Buy Their 3,000,000th Hybrid," *Hybrid Cars*, November 4, 2013, http://www.hybridcars.com/americans-buy-their-3000000th-hybrid/.

3. Ibid

4. "All-Electric Vehicles," US Department of Energy, Energy Efficiency & Renewable Energy, accessed June 2015, http://www.fueleconomy.gov/feg/evtech.shtml

5. Ibid.

6. Jim Ostroff, "Air Cars: A New Wind for America's Roads?" Kiplinger Washington Editors, Inc., October 30, 2008, http://finance.yahoo.com/family-home/ar-ticle/106040/Air-Cars:-A-New-Wind-for-America's-Roads.

7. "What You Can Do About Car Emissions," National Safety Council, February 27, 2008, http://www2.nsc.org/ehc/mobile/mse_fs.htm.

8. Clifford Krauss, "Driving Less, Americans Finally React to Sting of Gas Prices, a Study Says," *The New York Times*, June 20, 2008, http://biz.yahoo.com/nytimes/080620/1194786578804.html?.v=19.

9. Frank Newport, "Americans Convinced Rise in Gas Prices is Permanent," Gallup, May 9, 2008, http://www.gallup.com/poll/107170/Americans-Convinced-RiseGas-Prices-Permanent.aspx.

10. Krauss.

11. "What You Can Do About Car Emissions."

12. Michael Grunwald, "The Clean Energy Scam," *TIME*, April 7, 2008, 40–45.

13. Ibid.

14. Ibid.

15. Ibid.

16. Trystan L. Bass, "Drive-thrus are a waste," *Yahoo! Green*, January 18, 2008, http://green.yahoo.com/blog/greenpicks/101/drive-thrus-are-a-waste.html.

17. Ibid.

18. Ibid.

19. Trystan L. Bass, "Saving Gas Isn't Just For Tree-Huggers Anymore," *Yahoo! Green*, July 22, 2008, http://green.yahoo.com/blog/greenpicks/191/saving-gas-isn-t-justfor-tree-huggers-anymore.html.

CHAPTER NOTES

20. Joan Shim, "Six Ways to Stretch a Tank of Gas," *Yahoo! Green*, February 26, 2008, http://green.yahoo.com/blog/forecastearth/42/six-ways-to-stretch-a-tankof-gas.html.

21. Associated Press, "Bush Signs Bill Requiring 35 mpg Cars by 2020," *Columbia Tribune*, December 9, 2007, www.columbiatribune.com/2007/ dec/ 20071219News022.asp.

22. "Climate Change and President Obama's Action Plan," The White House, accessed June 2015, https://whitehouse.gov/climate-change.

Chapter 5. Greener Schools

1. Christy Radanof, interview, September 2008. Unless otherwise indicated, all quotes from Radanof come from this interview.

2. "Healthy Schools: School Buses," Environmental Association for Great Lakes Education, accessed October 2008, www.eagle-ecosource.org/buses.html.

3. "What Parents Need to Know about Diesel School Buses," Natural Resources Defense Council, March 17, 2001, www.nrdc.org/air/transportation/qbus.asp.

4. Dan Simon, "Reducing School Bus Emissions," *Greenworks TV*, September 10, 2002, www.greenworks.tv/radio/todaystory/20020910.htm.

5. "Going Green 101: Resources for Your Family," *The Oprah Winfrey Show*, April 20, 2007, www.oprah.com/article/oprahshow/tows_past_20070420_b.

6. "Myths About Energy in Schools: Energy Smart Schools," Energy Smart Schools Brochure: US Department of Energy, February 2002, www.nrel.gov/ docs/ fy02osti/31607.pdf.

7. "Energy Savings Tips for Schools," Alliance to Save Energy, accessed April 5, 2010, www.ase.org/ content/article/detail/625.

8. "School Operations and Maintenance: Best Practices for Controlling Energy Costs," Alliance to Save Energy, August 2004, www.ase.org/uploaded_files/ greenschools/School%20Energy%20Guidebook_9-04.pdf.

9. "Fun Facts about Saving Energy," Alliant Energy Kids, accessed June 2015, http:// www.alliantenergykids.com/EnergyandTheEnvironment/SavingEnergy/022393.

10. "Myths About Energy in Schools: Energy Smart Schools."

11. Ibid.

12. "Commercial Buildings: Schools," Building Technologies Program, US Department of Energy, September 25, 2009, www1.eere.energy.gov/buildings/commercial/schools.html.

13. "Green Power Solar Schools," Electric Cooperatives of South Carolina, accessed April 5, 2010, www.ecsc.org/index.php?option=com_content&task=view&id=178&Itemid=295.

14. "Myths About Energy in Schools: Energy Smart Schools."

15. Ibid.

16. "School Operations and Maintenance: Best Practices for Controlling Energy Costs."

Chapter 6. Greener Communities

1. Ben Feller, "Bush Hails Recovery of Tornado-leveled Kansas Town," *ABC News*, 2008, http://abcnews.go.com/Politics/Weather/wireStory?id=4782764.

2. "Devastated Kansas Town Goes Green," *ABC News*, August 15, 2007, http://abcnews.go.com/GMA/story?id=3481990&page=1.

3. Feller.

4. Associated Press, "After Twister, Greener Greensburg Rises," *MSNBC*, May 2, 2008, www.msnbc.msn.com/id/24416341/wid/18298287/.

5. Bryan Walsh, "Postcard: Greensburg. Building back from the rubble," *TIME*, March 17, 2008, 8.

6. "Devastated Kansas Town Goes Green."

7. "Recovery Plan," Official Web Site of Greensburg, Kansas, 2007, http://www.greensburgks.org/residents/recovery-planning/recovery-planning.

8. Associated Press, "After Twister, Greener Greensburg Rises."

9. Brett Zongker, "Greensburg featured in national museum," Kansas Rural Water Association, November 3, 2008, http://www.krwa.net/newsDB/MainAnnounce2.asp?key=448.

10. Ibid.

11. Associated Press, "After Twister, Greener Greensburg Rises."

12. "Devastated Kansas Town Goes Green."

13. "Issues: Smart Growth," Natural Resources Defense Council, accessed June 2015, http://www.nrdc.org/smartGrowth/visions/.

14. "Sustainable America," Civic Renewal Movement: CPN, accessed June 2015, http://clinton2.nara.gov/PCSD/Publications/suscomm/suscoint.html.

15. "Benefits for the Environment," Green Communities, accessed April 5, 2010, www.greencommunitiesonline.org/green/benefits/environment.asp.

16. "The ENERGY STAR for Buildings and Manufacturing Plants," *Energy Star*, accessed June 25, 2015, http://www.energystar.gov/index.cfm?c=business. bus_bldgs.

17. "Sustainable Community Examples," Rand Corporation, accessed June 2015, http://www.rand.org/pubs/monograph_reports/MR855/mr855.ch5.html.

18. "Vermont City Nabs Eco-Friendly Honor: Country Home Magazine Survey Cites 'Best Green Places' To Live in America," *CBS News*, March 8, 2007, http://www.cbsnews.com/news/vermont-city-nabs-eco-friendly-honor/.

19. Ibid.

20. Ibid.

21. Caryn Rousseau, "Chicago Outlines Plan to Slash Greenhouse Gases," September 19, 2008, www.enn.com/pollution/article/38231.

22. "How to Plant Trees to Conserve Energy for Summer Shade" Arbor Day Foundation, accessed June 2015, http://www.arborday.org/globalwarming/summerShade.cfm.

Chapter 7. Green or Grim Future? It's Up to You

1. "What We Know: The Reality, Risks, and Response to Climate Change" AAAS (Advancing Science, Serving Society), 2014, http://whatweknow.aaas.org/wp-content/uploads/2014/07/whatweknow_website.pdf.

2. Alex Nikolai Steffen, "The Next Green Revolution: How technology is leading environmentalism out of the anti-business, anti-consumer wilderness," *Wired*, 2009, www.wired.com/wired/archive/14.05/green_pr.html.

3. Ibid.

4. Naomi Klein, *This Changes Everything*, (New York: Simon & Schuster, 2014). 4

5. Ibid.

6. Ibid.

7. "Our Story," *Step It Up 2007*, accessed April 5, 2010, http://stepitup2007.org/article.php?list=type &type=48.

8. Ibid

9. Ibid.

10. Naomi Klein, "The Change Within: The Obstacles We Face Are Not Just External," *The Nation*, April 21, 2014, http://www.thenation.com/article/179460/change-within-obstacles-we-face-are-not-just-external#.

11. Manrodt, Alexis. "The New Face of Teen Activism," *Teen Vogue*, April 2014, http://www.teenvogue.com/my-life/2014-04/teen-online-activism.

12. Ibid.

13. Ibid.

14. "As U.S. Energy Production Grows, Public Policy Views Show Little Change," Pew Research Center: US Politics & Policy, December 18, 2014, http://www.people-press.org/2014/12/18/as-u-s-energy-production-grows-public-policy-views-show-little-change/.

15. Reliable Plant, "Americans Feel Energy Woes Won't Be Solved in Their Lifetime," accessed June 2015, http://www.reliableplant.com/Read/1670/americans-feel-energy-woes-won%27t-be-solved-in-ir-lifetime.

16. Klein, *This Changes Everything*, 452.

17. Ibid., 496.

GLOSSARY

biofuel—A type of fuel that is made from plant materials.

biomass—Natural material such as wood, paper, or waste that is used to make energy.

cap-and-trade system—A system that puts a cap, or limit, on how much carbon a company can produce; companies that produce less carbon can sell or trade to those who are over their limit.

carbon dioxide—A gas that is released into the atmosphere by both natural processes and human activities including driving, construction, daily living, and more; plants and trees store carbon dioxide.

carbon footprint—A calculation of how much carbon dioxide is released into the environment by an individual, a group, a building, or another entity.

carbon offset—A financial tool used to offset the size of a person's carbon footprint; an example would be paying to have trees planted as a way to offset the carbon a person puts into the air when driving a car.

climate change—A significant change in temperature as well as changes in wind and precipitation.

compressed air vehicle (CAV)—A car that works by compressing air instead of gasoline to move engine pistons.

daylighting—A process in which light is captured from the rooftop of a building and redirected to interior spaces.

deforestation—The process of cutting down and sometimes burning trees; increases carbon dioxide in the atmosphere.

emission—A substance discharged into the air.

energy vampires—Another name for electronic devices that use power even when they are turned off.

ethanol—A fuel made from corn kernels.

fossil fuel—Fuel that is made from the fossilized remains of things that died years ago; oil and coal are examples of fossil fuels.

fracking—Short for hydraulic fracturing, a type of drilling that injects liquid at high pressure into rocks to force open and extract oil or gas.

global warming—An increase in the average temperature of the earth's atmosphere.

greenhouse effect—A natural process in which some energy from the sun is absorbed and turned into heat to warm the earth. Global warming increases the greenhouse effect by making it harder for heat to be reflected back to the sun.

greenhouse gas—A gas found in the atmosphere, like carbon dioxide, that contributes to the greenhouse effect.

green power—Energy that provides the highest environmental benefit.

green pricing—The term refers to an optional utility service that allows customers to support a greater investment in renewable energy by paying a premium on their electric bill.

greenwashing—A term used to describe a company's methods to try to appear greener than it really is.

hybrid—A type of vehicle that has a battery-powered motor that works with a gasoline-powered engine to reduce the amount of fuel that is needed.

internal combustion engine (ICE)—A type of engine that is used for most vehicles; an engine in which fuel or gasoline is burned within the engine's cylinders.

nonrenewable energy—Resources that cannot be replaced, like oil and coal.

off-gas—Chemicals released into the air when a product is new.

renewable energy—Resources that can be replaced; unlike coal or oil, they will not run out; also called clean energy or green power.

sustainable—Capable of being continued with minimal long-term effect on the environment.

FOR MORE INFORMATION

Center for Biological Diversity's Generation Wild
biologicaldiversity.org/youth/

Includes information about programs, news, and events on a wide range of issues including climate change and sustainability as well as threats to the world's wildlife.

DoSomething.org
dosomething.org

Provides young people with the tools to get involved in all aspects of social change.

Earthforce, Inc.
earthforce.org

Encourages children and teens to be active citizens, improving the environment and the community.

SustainUS
sustainus.org

Dedicated to empowering young people to advance sustainable development.

TakingITGlobal
issues.tigweb.org/environment

Committed to helping youth from the around tackle global challenges

FURTHER READING

Clinton, Chelsea. *It's Your World: Get Informed, Get Inspired & Get Going!* New York: Philomel Books, 2015.

Fleischman, Paul. *Eyes Wide Open: Going Behind the Environmental Headlines.* Somerville, MA: Candlewick, 2014.

Gogerly, Liz. *A World After Fossil Fuels.* Chicago: Heinemann, 2013.

Haerens, Margaret, ed. *Energy Alternatives.* San Diego: Greenhaven Press, 2013.

Thompson, Laurie Ann. *Be a Changemaker: How to Start Something That Matters.* New York: Simon Pulse/Beyond Words, 2014.

INDEX